Special Praise for

DIRT ROADS & DINER PIE

"*Dirt Roads & Diner Pie* is filled with irony and humor, as well as heartbreaking, compassionate honesty. This is a story told with grace, and in Shonna's wise and loving words, it sings."

MORGAN CALLAN ROGERS
Author of ***Red Ruby Heart in a Cold Blue Sea*** and ***Written on My Heart***

"How many relationships end because the pain and shame of one's past is projected onto their partner? As a professional who specializes in childhood sexual trauma, as well as a survivor myself, *Dirt Roads & Diner Pie* chillingly illustrates how insidious sexual abuse can be, and how subtly it can deteriorate even a loving relationship.

"Reading this book was a rare opportunity to follow a couple on the brink and to sit in the backseat of a last-ditch-effort road trip to salvage their marriage. The love Humphrey has for her husband is evident in the tales of their journey, as is the exhaustion, frustration, and fear that stems from feeling helpless day after day. She presents an important reminder that the partners and family of childhood sexual abuse survivors are not on the sidelines—they are on the front lines. Humphrey also reminds the reader of the power of love, courage, commitment, and the willingness to walk through the darkness rather than run away from it. I appreciate that it wasn't happily ever after in the end, because past trauma never goes away. However, those living with trauma can learn to love themselves, and in the case of this story, so can their partners."

"If shame is the most toxic emotion, compassion and humor are the most powerful antidotes. Shonna Milliken Humphrey delivers both. Simultaneously soft-hearted and ferocious, she is the ideal guide to lead us across the broken ground of child sexual abuse."

"Every man who is able to have his story heard is not only taking an important step for his own recovery and healing but is also helping to protect future children from having to live through the same abuse. As the director of Male Survivor, the largest support organization for male survivors of sexual trauma, I fully endorse this book and Shonna's efforts to bring this issue into a broader, public conversation."

"Shonna Milliken Humphrey long has walked the difficult walk of the spouse of a sexual abuse victim. She has now extended a much-needed hand to others in her shoes and opened a large window of understanding needed by the rest of us."

DIRT ROADS & DINER PIE

Dirt Roads
& DINER PIE

One Couple's Road Trip to Recovery
from Childhood Sexual Abuse

SHONNA MILLIKEN HUMPHREY

CENTRAL RECOVERY PRESS

Las Vegas

Central Recovery Press (CRP) is committed to publishing exceptional materials addressing addiction treatment, recovery, and behavioral healthcare topics.

For more information, visit www.centralrecoverypress.com.

Publisher: Central Recovery Press
3321 N. Buffalo Drive
Las Vegas, NV 89129

21 20 19 18 17 16   1 2 3 4 5

Names: Humphrey, Shonna Milliken, author.
Title: Dirt roads and diner pie : one couple's road trip to recovery from childhood sexual abuse / Shonna Milliken Humphrey.
Description: Las Vegas : Central Recovery Press, 2016.
Identifiers: LCCN 2016006393 (print) | LCCN 2016019801 (e-book) | ISBN 9781942094227 (paperback) | ISBN 9781942094234 (e-book)
Subjects: LCSH: Adult child sexual abuse victims—Family relationships—United States. | Child sexual abuse—Psychological aspects. | Humphrey, Shonna Milliken—Travel—Southern States. | Humphrey, Travis James—Travel—Southern States. | Travel—Psychological aspects. | Married people—United States—Biography. | Adult child sexual abuse victims—United States—Biography. | Humphrey, Travis James—Childhood and youth. | Sexually abused boys—New Jersey—Princeton—Biography. |American Boychoir School—History. | BISAC: BIOGRAPHY & AUTOBIOGRAPHY / Personal Memoirs. | FAMILY & RELATIONSHIPS / Abuse / Child Abuse. |PSYCHOLOGY / Psychopathology / Post-Traumatic Stress Disorder (PTSD). |FAMILY & RELATIONSHIPS / Conflict Resolution.
Classification: LCC HV6570.2 .H857 2016 (print) | LCC HV6570.2 (e-book) | DDC 362.76092/273 [B] —dc23
LC record available at https://lccn.loc.gov/2016006393

Photo of Shonna Milliken Humphrey by Erin Irish. Used with permission.

Excerpt of "Now" from *The Executive Director of the Fallen World* by Liam Rector, published by the University of Chicago Press. Reprinted with permission of the University of Chicago Press.

Every attempt has been made to contact copyright holders. If copyright holders have not been properly acknowledged, please contact us. Central Recovery Press will be happy to rectify the omission in future printings of this book.

Cover design and interior by Marisa Jackson.

FOR ELISABETH WILKINS LOMBARDO

who ranked among my husband's greatest champions

AUTHOR'S NOTE

———

While this memoir chronicles an actual month-long United States road trip, I have adjusted some names and identifying details to protect the privacy of family and friends. Where appropriate, these instances are identified within the context of the narrative. Conversations and event sequences are expressed in service to the narrative and to the best of my recollection.

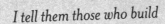

I tell them those who build

And master are the ones invariably
Merry: Give and take quarter,
Create good meals within the slaughter,

A place for repose and laughter
In the consoling beds of being tender

———

Excerpt from "Now" by Liam Rector

PROLOGUE
The Beginning

"Just don't make it one of those douche-y, 'look-at-me' confessionals," Trav requested when this book moved from an idea to words on paper.

I nodded.

"And try not to make me sound like a jackass."

I nodded again.

"And make it funny."

"Got it," I said. "A funny memoir about childhood sexual abuse where your character is the opposite of a jackass." Thinking of the most suave and socially adept figures in film and literature, I suggested modeling Trav's persona after Humphrey Bogart's Rick Blaine or Ian Fleming's James Bond.

"Magnum, P.I., would be okay, too."

This is how the conversation devolved into a review of which fictional good guy Trav would choose to lead a military-style extraction team: MacGyver, Thomas Magnum, Michael Knight, James Bond, or Cordell Walker.

After some debate, MacGyver won.

"Would your answer change if the A-Team was an option?"

"Obviously."

As always, these absurd exchanges make me laugh, but Trav's extensive knowledge of iconic television, literary, and film heroes is no accident. For thirty months from 1988 to 1990, he was unable to sleep because of the sex abuse he saw, heard, feared, and experienced as a student at the American Boychoir School. He sought brave, strong, and honorable male archetypes in fiction because none of those heroes materialized in real life.

Instead of summoning a talking car or a Walther PPK, Trav began drinking coffee at age eleven to remain alert and vigilant during the nighttime hours.

CHAPTER ONE
Between Desire & Piety

New Orleans is a crooked city, and those comforted by right angles quickly become disoriented. Given that New Orleans sinks, by some estimations, one-half inch each year, a walk down any side street is a study in hodgepodge and a test of one's inner compass. Exteriors are plastered behind balconies that list and buckle. Cars dodge uneven cobblestone and brick potholes. Grave markers, too, settle into the ground, swallowed up by the damp earth.

"Northern Caribbean climate," a tour guide explained, and I noted the situational irony that we had left Maine to escape the stormy weather, but instead of feeling warm Caribbean sun on our faces, we huddled in knitted hats and rubbed our hands together, wishing we had packed mittens.

It was a metaphor for our marriage—not what I expected—and I avoided extending the metaphor as we stood in the crumbles of the

St. Louis Cemetery during one of the coldest and wettest February days on record. I stared at the statue whose lap Dennis Hopper scaled during the acid-fueled filming of *Easy Rider*, imagining the sensation of being cradled in those smooth, white marble arms. Homer Plessy's French-inscribed monument stood farther back, not far from the incongruity of actor Nicolas Cage's pre-purchased modern pyramid.

"So much history," I whispered, and drew another connection to our marriage. It was impossible not to lament the beautifully sculpted maze of tombs slowly shifting even deeper below sea level, and I felt as depressed as the stones themselves.

Imagine a husband who winces when touched. Even the smallest physical gesture is a loaded experience. While many people try not to think about their husbands' past sex lives, for partners like me that avoidance gets multiplied by a thousand. I understood Trav would likely have had experiences before we met. It was part, I reasoned, of a healthy self.

I was not prepared for childhood sexual trauma, and it is difficult to reconcile the strong, broad-shouldered, muscular, and tattooed man I married existing in such a vulnerable state, immersed in a culture of sexual manipulation and violence.

After the cemetery tour, I licked a thick powdered-sugar coating from a hot beignet at Café Du Monde as the rain pelted the café's outdoor-seating tent flaps. A woman at the next table pulled the price tags from fuzzy striped socks she had just purchased and then removed her shoes to slip them over her bare, pink feet. The servers, mostly elderly men and women, hustled in their paper caps, and the uniforms seemed as sad and undignified as the shivering saxophone player's cold fingers producing a tinny version of "Down by the Riverside" for the tourist crowd.

I could not shake the cemetery malaise, and the sense that this was my trajectory—heavy, cold, sinking, gray, and lonely. I wanted to reach across the table for Trav's hand to feel connected to something warm and good, but I suspected he would pull it away.

As if to emphasize the moment, two smiling honeymooners stood in my sightline, and the young man pushed dark, rain-soaked curls from his forehead and kissed his wife's wedding ring. She looked up toward the canvas ceiling and laughed, balancing her cup with an outstretched arm. I imagined this dismal weather was an adventure for them, their marriage new, and he drew her waist into his. The young woman's cheeks flushed at the motion, and her long, dark hair moved forward to cover her face. As he did with his own curls, the man combed back his wife's bangs and touched her cheek, whispering, "I love you."

Trav would never do that.

He would never bring my waist into his for a spontaneous neck nuzzle, and after watching this young couple's happiness, I no longer had an appetite for the sugary little doughnuts on the plate in front of me.

"Are you going to finish those?" Trav asked, and I nudged the plate closer to him.

"All for you."

There was something so sensuous about the young couple admiring their new wedding rings on a frigid, rainy day, something primal in the gesture of the young man pushing back his new wife's hair. I envied that woman, and I wanted to feel a man's hands touch me with desire.

———

For years, Trav had backpedaled my assessment. It was, he said, a problem of my own making. I was too needy and too demanding, and my requests were too much. *Oversexed* was the word that stung most.

This perception is common among sex abuse survivors.

It is easy for a sex abuse survivor to assign blame, and it is especially easy for a partner to feel ashamed of her (or his) sexual self. This can prompt a cycle of diminished self-esteem, and for the two of us, it is among the toughest aspects of healing to negotiate.

For a long time, there was little welcome initiation for Trav.

———

So, when a former boyfriend of mine reached out with a "how are you doing," my answer skewed defensive. His question might be innocuous, or it might be suggestive. *What did he know?* I wondered. It was not the first time I had interacted with former boyfriends, and I lacked a good response.

"Okay" did not seem accurate.

It feels strange and uncomfortable to discuss sex issues outside our marriage, and it feels disloyal to remember any charged sexual history with other men. It feels worse to enjoy the way an ex's gaze affirms that I do still look good—and it feels abysmal to consider any possibility of a discreet arrangement.

Each time I encountered a man like this, I offered a casual air-kiss and quick hug, but I also calculated logistics, risk, and reward. I sketched out how it might play out, and, shamed, tried to redirect my own perceptions.

Still, it is impossible for partners not to consider.

If I am not connected physically to Trav, I thought, *what role do I play?* The job titles nurse, mother, cook, accountant, assistant, and friend felt fundamentally bare.

Since neither Trav nor I had requested these issues, I found myself wondering again how I had acquired this particular set of circumstances.

I married a man who grew up six houses away from my childhood home in rural northern Maine. I watched chubby, redheaded Trav pedal his bicycle for the length of our shared street, never imagining that we would meet as adults in the most random circumstance while both living in Washington, DC. I never imagined that after dating for approximately two weeks we would decide to share an apartment, and one year later he would become my husband. If someone had told me I would marry a survivor of institutionalized, prolonged, systemic child sexual abuse, I would not have believed it.

And if these details seemed fantastic, I *really* could not predict a body pillow dividing my bed for more than a decade and a machete stationed by the nightstand. "My husband doesn't like to touch me" is a phrase I never thought I would repeat while sitting on a therapist's couch, either.

"I did not sign up for this" is a common refrain, and I suspect many partners like me inhale sharply, wondering how they got to this place, feeling bitter and weary, too.

———

For the first year of our marriage, sex with Trav was frequent, varied, energetic, and fantastic. We once spent an entire twenty-four hours in bed, broke a restroom sink with our enthusiasm, and stopped the car en route to a friend's wedding. He loved my red silk robe, but he preferred it balled up on the floor.

We were equally matched, and I entered the relationship feeling informed and lucky. As Trav grew comfortable, faced his history, and sought treatment, that is when the dark phase began. Trav began to heal, but he retreated sexually.

However, that assessment feels skewed because when he is in the right headspace, I have zero complaints. It just takes so much effort to reach that headspace sometimes.

In what I imagine is another common scenario for partners like me, I feel selfish for supporting his healing but also thinking, *What about me?*

———

When Trav asked me to write our story, this is where things got complicated. Trav was the boy who was abused, but his abuse affects nearly every aspect of my life, too. "Our" story is muddy.

To co-opt his experience is wrong, to deny the effects untruthful. Partners like me are often left on the sidelines, watching the effects of childhood sexual abuse play out on the field of our husbands' psyches—a field where there is little room for our own selves.

"I am glad this happened to me and not you," Trav mused at the New Orleans café table when his coffee cup was empty. He paused before finishing his thought, skimming the ceramic handle with his thumb.

"Knowing that someone hurt my wife would be so much worse."

CHAPTER TWO
Estimated Time of Departure

A week or so before we made it to New Orleans, on the morning of our month-long Americana road trip departure, I was stuck in a state of ennui. Last-minute packing, cleaning, and shopping topped my to-do list, but my body stayed weighted and listless under a heavy quilt. The words in my head: overwhelmed, tired, sad, lonely, and angry.

These were all abstractions—intangible words that cannot be tasted, touched, seen, or heard, and I regularly encouraged creative writing students to avoid them. Much better, I taught, are concrete examples. Abstractions are vague non-descriptors, and I illustrate this in my classroom by requesting immediate associations for "love."

Kittens! My boyfriend! Jesus! Chocolate! My baby! These always topped the responses, and I spoke about command of language and craft. "Do you," I asked, "want to use a word that elicits such a varied reader response?"

It is always better to use specifics: a blue-edged teacup, a banana peel, or the corn-chip scent of an Australian shepherd puppy paw.

As I burrowed deeper into the blankets, I knew my abstractions were dull, but the concrete expressions felt too depressing: Maine winter temperatures drop to −32°F. My husband must consume six prescription drugs daily. One of our dogs died last month. As a child in the care of the American Boychoir School, Trav experienced a level of sex abuse that profoundly affects all aspects of his—and therefore my—adult life.

My concrete expressions were vivid, but heavy. I dug even farther under the covers, thinking about the conversation from the night before.

———

Trav and I sat at opposite ends of our couch on a strangely warm day in late January with a thermometer reading in the upper thirties that prompted a pseudospring of melting ice and felt like the cruelest sort of joke in a state with fifteen hours of daily winter darkness that does not grow consistent green grass until May.

"Is this how couples break up?" he asked.

We had reached a life stage where it seemed like every month a different friend or family member announced a split.

Trav poured himself a cup of coffee, and he refreshed my tea water from our orange kettle. He would leave soon for his last nighttime performance before our road trip, and I had already been home from campus for an hour. I brought takeout food, but like his tea water refresh, it seemed like the smallest of gestures. Winter and ambivalence overwhelmed us both.

———

Trav is a musician, and I am a writer. Having managed opposite schedules since we first met, when we find ourselves in a rare moment of overlapping time, we are generally direct and honest in our assessments.

He continued, facing forward with no eye contact. "I can see why some couples divorce."

The *divorce* word gave me pause, not because I wasn't thinking it myself, but because I did not know it was on Trav's mind.

Our tactic had always been to let situations breathe, but that night on the couch felt absent of oxygen. I studied his strong and muscular features—after all these years, a familiar silhouette. He wore a flannel shirt and jeans, sock-footed, with his boots beside the coffee table. In profile, I watched him sip from his mug and unwrap his veggie focaccia sandwich, a sandwich I have ordered for him a hundred times. Salt and pepper, no mayonnaise.

The word *divorce* felt like a test in the way canaries were used in old coal mines, and I considered my reaction.

It had been a rough year.

Trav went public with the sex abuse he had endured while studying at the American Boychoir School, and the anger and the repercussions reverberated through our marriage until the noise was so loud, I could no longer hear. For Trav, getting through the day was a win, and sleeping through the night was a gold medal.

———

Once Trav's vague memories of his time as a choirboy became more detailed, the details did not stop. This afternoon he remembered the effects of his friend's most violent rape. It was the worst to date. He coped by doing fifty hard push-ups after telling me. Finding no physical release, he smashed an old dartboard with a hammer until the noise scared our dog. I brought him an antianxiety pill, and we sat together.

This is what post-traumatic stress disorder looks like in our house.

"Why didn't I tell anyone?" he asked.

"Because you were a little boy, had no language, and did not feel safe," I said. It was a small comfort, and when the first pill did not work, he swallowed more until his words slurred.

Compounding the issue, Trav had misjudged the time and was due onstage in two hours.

"Do you think you can perform?" I asked, glancing at the clock.

"If I am seated, yes."

Placing a warm washcloth on Trav's neck, I visualized the dim, rear-corner stage setup. The venue was a blues bar, and the show was a power lounge trio. Trav had worked this spot regularly for more than a year, and since the bar staff loved him, they would cut him some slack for a seated performance.

"B.B. King performed seated," I joked. "You are channeling your blues master roots."

Though alert enough to pack his own equipment, Trav was in no way able to drive. I left a heads-up message with the bass player who booked the gig, and as I piloted the van into town, I asked Trav to sing to me.

His voice projected well, and he remembered most of the lyrics. This was a comfort.

The drummer met us at the curb, saw Trav's nodding head, and left to find coffee. I thanked him, grateful for the discretion and absence of questions.

Trav righted his shoulders and inhaled deeply. He opened the passenger-side door and stepped onto the curb. A bartender on a smoke break greeted him with a hearty handshake, and Trav walked inside, smiling, steady, and not stumbling.

———

By the time I returned after midnight to drive him home, I had baked three apple pies from scratch as stress relief. While the pies bubbled in the oven, with a full name from Trav's afternoon memory now attached to the most sadistic perpetrator, I searched online and learned that the man, a social studies and physical education teacher just like Trav's fuzzy recollections suggested but could not confirm, was arrested and charged with aggravated sexual assault that had occurred in November of 1989, one year into Trav's education.

The only media attention I could locate was on page ten of a Princeton community newspaper, on the bottom of the page next to a camera advertisement. It noted a single isolated incident and a single victim. Later, this faculty member was punished with a $430 fine and four years of probation.[1]

"One instance? One perpetrator? One victim?" Trav would respond the next morning when I shared the research, disgust in his voice.

———

As I drove to pick him up after the show, the scent of cinnamon and pastry crust covered the van's usual plastic cable, dog, and cigar smoke

1   *https://archive.org/stream/towntopicsprince4601unse#page/10/mode/2up*

odor. I inhaled and exhaled the apple pie scent with intention, still debating whether to share the court information, wondering if the details would validate his new memories or create an even worse headspace. The murky recollections that plagued Trav's memory were confirmed by my research, but I had no idea whether this confirmation would help or hurt the situation.

I parked the van by the curb; Trav stood waiting in the venue vestibule. He had sobered up, and when he slid his guitar into the vehicle, his face reflected shame despite the guys making light as I handed them the still-warm pie pans through the window.

"You are living the life, my friend!" they joked. "A hot chauffeur with homemade dessert!"

I gave a thumbs-up as Trav settled into the seat, wondering how much—if anything—these band guys knew. No fans noticed any difference in the performance quality, Trav said, but he would later thrash himself awake and upright in the early morning hours, sweating next to me. On instinct, I reached my arm over the body pillow that had divided our bed since we moved in together. I rubbed his shoulder and coaxed him to breathe.

"Shhh," I whispered. "You're okay."

In the predawn hours, I repeated the words. "You're okay."

Eventually Trav's breathing became regular, as it always does. That is the beauty of his current combination of medications: The night terrors still happen, but he doesn't always remember them.

CHAPTER THREE
Push Away the Blanket

"I need for the Boychoir to not take up so much space in our life," I said on the night before our trip. It felt like an ultimatum, but I knew it was an empty one. With fourteen years invested, and a genuine affection for this man, I had no "or else" plan.

However, childhood sexual abuse affected our conversations, our family interactions, and our physical health. Our marital routine had become a slow mental drag, and it was hard to sort a typical ebb from the sinister undercurrent. Communications read like boring interview questions. Did you remember to feed the cats? Do we have enough money in the account? Can you get the mail? Did you sleep okay?

That last one, the sleep question, was the biggie. It plagued us. Since the early days of our marriage, Trav had battled night terrors in a cycle of not sleeping, being afraid to sleep, sweat-inducing nightmares, and then more not sleeping. He regularly shakes himself upright in our bed, and sometimes he screams.

"It stresses me out when, every morning, you ask if I slept well," he eventually confessed. "I will never sleep well."

I nodded as if I could possibly understand and promised to limit that topic.

———

I do not remember who made the decision to spend four weeks in pursuit of Americana and creative inspiration while leaving the snow-filled, icy Maine February behind us, but we agreed it was a good idea.

My hope was to shift the energy between us and push a reset button. What felt like the millionth pharmaceutical approach to his sleeplessness seemed to be helping, and I wanted to rid ourselves of distractions, get on a consistent schedule, forget work, and eat good food. I wanted to remember why I chose to spend my life with this man, and most of all, I wanted to not think about the Boychoir every single day.

"I am serious," I said. "This trip will make or break us."

———

Still, on our departure morning, I could not get out of bed. The house felt strange with our travel items neatly packed by the door and the smell of furniture polish permeating the freshly dusted room.

"I don't want to go," I whined from underneath the blankets. Anxiety levels rose in my chest, and I ran down the scenarios in my head: The house could burn, my sister might need me, our parents could get hurt, or the cats could die. Fear was a choker around my neck, and I tried to mitigate the fear with rational thoughts.

From under the covers, I remembered the last time we had traveled. It was to California for a wedding, and on our last day in San Francisco, Trav paced the hotel room in anticipation of the return flight. This pacing happens every time we travel. Any situation that removes control—particularly losing all control during the heat and swell of the airport, the tight and claustrophobic squeeze into the plane, and sitting immobile for several hours in flight—is a misery for my husband. Many people do not enjoy flying, but for Trav, the panic is more sinister.

It taps into time he spent as an American Boychoir student that was filled with unfamiliar and dangerous experiences, unreliable adults, and a need for an extreme level of hypervigilance to protect himself.

We had ten hours until departure, so I suggested we drive through the city and visit Golden Gate Park's Japanese Tea Garden. He loves spaces with positive, Zen-focused energy.

Something to offer him control, I have learned, works well. Focusing on the car, the streets, and the directions helps. But on that day, Trav gripped the steering wheel, his triceps tight.

Despite the peaceful nature of the lush space, Trav could not focus. He had no energy to traverse the inchworm-like wooden bridge or contemplate the fat orange koi, and had no appetite for a teahouse snack. We burned time with some stale éclairs at a neighborhood bakery.

"Can we please just go to the airport and get it over with?"

By then it was noon, and our flight left at 8:00 P.M.

I dosed Trav with an antianxiety pill in the car rental return area, and then another in the terminal. Tucked way back in the farthest corner so no other passengers could see his shaking, he drank whiskey at the airport bar.

When I handed him two antihistamines just before boarding, he asked for three.

For the next six in-flight hours I watched his rigid body, face forward and clinging to the armrests.

That is my job, I often think. Watching Trav. As a performer, Trav gets paid to have people watch him, but I was sick of the task.

————

Once so optimistically planned, on the morning of departure this road trip felt like a month-long slog of watching Trav, caring for Trav, and participating in a Trav-focused parade of Trav-issues. I felt unequipped for the task.

But our dog had been delivered to my in-laws. Trav's sister would feed the cats. The contractors intended to use our time away to remodel the rotten bathroom in our 1961 Cape. The basement mold-abatement estimate came in, and the company promised to start work as soon as we returned.

Plans had been made, and Trav packed the van while I shrugged off the quilt.

CHAPTER FOUR
First Corinthians

The drive south from Maine is ugliest in February. Any brief peek of ocean shows it foamy with garbage. Roadside snow is hard packed and covered by sand, ice, and gravel. Rather than offering sun-soaked summer blue-water views, Maine moved through New Hampshire and into Massachusetts via a constant screen of crumbling-brick mill smokestacks with clusters of vinyl-sided houses standing close to the highway.

I wondered about those houses and whether the highway came first and the homeowners received a special incentive to build, or the houses were grandfathered in tight when the highway was made. Apartments were stacked on top of each other in the multiunit structures, and squat ranches and awkward split-levels represented the single-family houses. After taking a mental note to research the highway's history, I quickly forgot.

To pass the first day of drive time, I made up elaborate stories about the occupants of those homes visible from the highway, imagining torn linoleum kitchen floors, the smell of heavy diapers, and mothers cooking generic boxed macaroni and cheese for a crowd of dirty-faced children. After passing house after house with cracked, mint-colored siding and broken plastic toys strewn across the frozen mud-and-snow-covered yards, I stopped with the character development because all my stories were sad.

We drove past gray-and-brown strip mall backsides, too, in differing states of decay, as well as half-done construction projects with massive piles of dirt and idle yellow equipment.

I wanted to note something beautiful, like stark, bare tree branches resembling lace with their bent limbs and intricate patterns against the clouds, but it was just a gray-and-brown road blur against gray-and-brown structures under a gray-and-brown sky.

A hot-pink Dunkin' Donuts coffee-mobile car pulled up beside us and broke the view of dull highway, and the driver waved at me from the next lane. I waved back through the window while sipping hot tea and thinking about omens and luck. That bright pink car with its oversized Styrofoam cup-shaped attachment seemed like an omen: frivolous and happy. Trav and I had the entire month of February to check out, move off the grid, and find sun. That felt like the best kind of luck.

We had saved money for this trip, and each Sunday that we shared pizza instead of sitting across a cloth-covered table spread with briny Damariscotta River oysters or a big bowl of savory Tsukimi Udon, I imagined the savings buying us Nashville biscuits and New Orleans beignets. Now that we were officially on the road, I dug into the bag of sliced green apples from the snack box between our seats and balanced my boots on the dashboard.

————

"You are patient," I said to Trav on that first day of driving, and I still do not know what prompted that observation. He is, though. It is a trait I do not share. Trav can step back, smile, and assess a situation with a sense of perspective and comfort.

"It is adaptive," Trav answered, but I disagreed.

"I think it is innate."

I watched Trav's face as he drove, and I watched his body, too. Had I not been present, his approach would be more aggressive, and I appreciated his effort to drive slower and with more deliberation, a nod to my comfort, as the traffic got thicker.

He handles vehicles well, and his steady hands rested on the bottom of the steering wheel after pulling a pair of aviator sunglasses from the pocket of his well-worn hooded sweatshirt. The highway billboards—illegal in Maine—popped up in abundance as we sped through Massachusetts. The initial set advertised junk cars for sale, then an Army recruiting station, and when the first religious message appeared, it was a Bible verse.

First Corinthians. "Love is patient."

Having just noted Trav's patience, I thought this, too, seemed like an omen.

Trav laughed when I said I preferred the alternative translation of "Love suffers long."

"Semantics," he said.

It felt like a good sign.

CHAPTER FIVE
New Jersey Legal

At the exact moment we left the New England states and diverted onto the New Jersey Turnpike, Trav's neck stiffened. It was a subtle change, and I doubt another person would have noticed. My feet still rested on the dashboard, and although I had long finished the hot tea from Maine, I continued to fiddle with the empty paper cup.

The New Jersey portion was a blip on our trip's overall itinerary, but it took up the most mental space. It is a simple marker, the line into New Jersey, but neither of us spoke because there were no good words. New Jersey is loaded with significance.

———

Trav described his first arrival in Newark at age eleven as one of chaos. An unaccompanied minor in the pre-mobile phone era, he got lost in the airport and, until located, spent his time wandering the terminals alone.

"What did you do?" I asked.

"I don't remember," he said, "but I must have found a pay phone and called someone."

———

Photos of the American Boychoir School's historic Albemarle campus building façade match Trav's memory: a wide circular driveway, eight portico columns, and five dormered windows on the third floor. Trav described the 1917 estate in remarkable detail, and photos align against his details with an eerie level of accuracy. In one image is the formal staircase where he learned to maintain a military-style formation line before descending at each mealtime. He described the sharp creases in his uniform: navy blue pants, white shirt, and red sweater.

When Trav lived at the Albemarle campus in Princeton, classes were conducted in a series of rooms on the first and third floors. Because the choir traveled often, classes also happened in the tour bus. He learned science and math, social studies and language arts.

When not on tour, Trav practiced choral music every day in a high-ceilinged open space called "The Loggia." For a little boy raised in a modest home, Italian architectural vocabulary felt foreign and overwhelming.

"The Loggia," he repeated softly when he told me.

Albemarle's physical details also included the second-floor living spaces. Occupancy varied according to age, and in Trav's first year he bunked with eight boys. Their bedroom connected directly to an overnight staff perpetrator's room, and Trav remembers trying to sleep through the sounds from behind that particular room's door, wondering if and when he might be next.

Stretching behind the school itself, a manicured, formal field extended toward a natural spring-fed pool with freezing-cold water where Trav would swim. Beyond this pool was a stand of forest where Trav hollowed out a place in the thicket to crouch and hide.

Trav described laundry facilities in a dark basement and a strange hallway-cupboard storage space on the main floor. The former he avoided at all costs, and the latter he converted into another secret hiding place.

Late at night, Trav snuck into the school's kitchen and ate dry cereal by the handful.

"Well," I said. "That might explain your current late-night food compulsions."

———

I suspect many people have no idea about the pervasive and long-lasting nature of childhood sexual abuse, and this lack of awareness is among the hardest parts to navigate because no lawsuit, apology, or jail time will ever make things right. We both wanted some form of understanding, though, so when Trav gave me permission to contact the school, I struggled to find the right words.

I had long ago requested that the American Boychoir School stop sending us solicitation letters, and they did; so, I proceeded with the good-faith assumption that honest conversations can resolve most issues. Since the American Boychoir School had participated in a court case,[2] however reluctantly, that helped change child sexual abuse laws,

2 HARDWICKE V. AMERICAN BOYCHOIR SCHOOL. *Decided August 8, 2006.*
   http://caselaw.findlaw.com/nj-supreme-court/1138661.html

I expected them to be, if not leaders on the topic, at least willing to discuss the issues.

Given the long history of allegations about the school, I also expected there would be a basic protocol for reporting, resources, and reparation.

I was naïve.

Trav and I have a friend who practices law locally, and before I contacted the school I asked her informally about the best process for obtaining some form of apology. Instead of meeting over our usual coffee, our lawyer friend invited us both to her office. Her tone was grave, and she wanted us to fully understand the process.

Her space, warm and inviting with exposed brick walls, antique wooden fixtures, and natural light from tall windows, overlooked a small park in Portland's Old Port district. Sitting at her conference table, we learned about criminal action and civil action.

In simplest and most reductive terms, criminal charges happen with a goal of jail time for the perpetrator. Civil action holds a person or an organization responsible for damages, almost always financially. Both put the burden of proof on the party who claims he or she was wronged. In a criminal proceeding, proof must be beyond a reasonable doubt. With civil charges, the burden is known as "preponderance of the evidence" or, in numerical shorthand, 51 percent. This is a key distinction. Civil cases must demonstrate it is *more likely than not* that a person or organization is responsible.

Our friend explained that the first step in a civil proceeding is to send a demand letter. Although this is a mean-sounding term, a demand letter outlines the circumstance and invites a conversation.

"Great!" Trav and I agreed. A letter seemed perfect! We would include a statement from Trav's doctors to demonstrate our legitimacy with more than ten years of documented treatment, and we would start a conversation—exactly what we wanted.

That is when our lawyer friend said that if we sent this letter, we must be prepared to enter litigation.

"Say more," we requested. Neither of us is stupid, but *litigation* was a word we generally heard only on televised court dramas.

The school, she explained, would likely give any demand letter directly to an insurance company. Since insurance companies often handle these situations, an institution typically extracts itself from any active participation.

"Huh," we thought, confused. "That doesn't seem right."

What she described next was worse.

The insurance company would likely deny any claims, forcing us to bring a lawsuit. If we sued, the next step would be "discovery," during which Trav would be required to disclose not just his own experiences, but any rapes witnessed by him or confided to him by other little boys, including names and any available contact information. This disclosure would bolster his credibility, and Trav would be asked to list each specific act of sexual misconduct he recalled and experienced, assigning dates, times, and identifying details for verification.

What's more, Trav's therapist, psychiatrist, and physician would likely be compelled to submit all session notes and patient files, and every private conversation would be used by a team of insurance litigators to discredit him.

Any mention of sexual dysfunction, any suicidal consideration, any medications tried, and any moment of marital or personal doubt would be scrutinized for inconsistencies. My husband's entire collection of private physical and psychological details would be open to a roomful of professionals paid to cast doubt on his already shaky, twenty-five-year-old boyhood recollections.

"Just for an apology?" I asked.

"This could get very ugly," our lawyer friend explained, noting that civil cases often last for years.

Perversely, Trav's personal success would count against him. "How bad can his life really be," a litigator might ask, "if Trav is able to work full time? If he owns a home? If he has never been arrested? If his credit score is good? If he is widely respected in his community? If he can maintain a marriage and friendships?"

"The school is aware of its history," I countered. "Can we just send statements that show the severity of his situation?" I moved my head toward the window's park view for a moment, the lush green grass color intensified by the overcast sky, as I tried to negotiate a saner alternative, because the system our friend described made no sense.

A statement from Trav's doctors that summarized treatment details with dates seemed ample proof for a "preponderance" that, more likely than not, spending thirty sleepless months hearing, seeing, avoiding, and experiencing already-documented child sexual abuse is the source of his post-traumatic stress disorder.

And, once that was established, why wouldn't the school officials say, "I am sorry this happened while you were in our care. How can we help?"

When I turned back toward Trav, his face had reddened, his breathing was shallow, and his eyes were glassy. There was no space for push-ups, and if he had had a hammer, he would have pounded it.

I wanted Trav to find his voice, but that day in our lawyer friend's conference room, I imagined my own deepest, most shameful secrets and darkest memories not just being exposed, but exposed to a team of strangers whose professional mission is to discredit details, line by line, and I began to respect the strength many victims find in silence.

I put my hand on Trav's and thanked our friend for the information. We both hugged her and made vague plans to meet for dinner. Then we drove home.

———

As for so many victims, Trav's options for justice and reparation are nearly nonexistent.

On one side is an institution with a well-documented, decades-long history of childhood sexual abuse allegations, and on the other side my husband juggles more than a decade of documented post-traumatic stress in an effort to function. For a 51 percent likelihood that the two are related, this seemed like an easy correlation.

It sounds fair, but it is common for men who suffer from childhood sexual abuse-related post-traumatic stress disorder to bury memories deep. While specific statistics vary, childhood sexual abuse cases, especially among boys, are vastly underreported and rarely see legal action. Statutes of limitation vary in intricacy and by state; financial settlements can be taxed as income, and generally speaking, 30 percent is paid to a personal-injury lawyer.

Most importantly, while in litigation and often as a settlement condition, nobody involved can talk or write publicly about the topic.

The invasive and prolonged discovery process is a tactic likely meant to avert false accusations. False accusations are a fear, but false accusations are also exceedingly rare and account for approximately 1–2 percent of all accusations. Victims tend to *understate,* rather than *overstate,* their experience, and many victims are reluctant to take their cases to court.

Shame, fear, and lack of basic vocabulary contribute to underreporting in children. For adults—especially and exponentially among male victims—it is not facing the perpetrators; it is the lead-up to the process. For men, it's often less about fearing the perpetrators (as it is with children) and more about dealing with the machinations of the justice system. A large majority of victims lock memories away in an effort to survive. Recollections often emerge slowly and in dim fragments over time. For anyone attempting to hold an individual or, worse, an entire institution responsible, those fragments do not feel convincing.

It is a cycle that perpetuates itself: Shame and lack of vocabulary for children result in shame and buried memories for adults.

"I might not have the timeline and details 100 percent," Trav maintains. "But I know what I saw, and I know what I heard." And, most heartbreakingly, "I know what happened to me."

As his wife, I needed to know that I had brought Trav every option for his consideration. I could not do push-ups or pound a hammer, but I could find the best experts for the best advice. I could bring my husband choices.

I contacted a second lawyer—one who represented other alumni in other sexual-abuse cases against the American Boychoir School. This lawyer confirmed our friend's explanation, and his ease with the process was equal parts disarming and reassuring. He asked what Trav's medical records would indicate, and more importantly, when.

What and when?

They seem like simple questions, but again, the answers are much more complex. I draw a line of accountability from my husband to the institution tasked with keeping him safe, but legally, this line gets wiggly. If, for example, Trav spent a weekend at the home of a trustee, off campus and out of state, but the perpetrator was the trustee's *colleague* and not the trustee himself, that abuse would likely not "count."

Being afraid to sleep while resisting sexual advances by staff and teachers or witnessing the repeated sexual abuse of other boys? This is difficult, too, because as with the damage caused by secondhand smoke, those sleepless months were harmful, but were they caused by *actual* sexual abuse or *fear* of sexual abuse? The former is a straight line, and the latter is not.

Any sexual activity among students—even older students acting out their own abuses by faculty and staff members on younger boys—could be considered consensual and age-appropriate experimentation.

The Boychoir traveled extensively throughout the United States and Europe, spending nights with random, unvetted host families, and laws governing childhood sexual abuse differed in each location. Compounding the confusion, Trav was barely eleven years old and often only remembers first names or no names at all.

The "when" is even more laughable. His clinical depression, when first diagnosed? Or the first inklings of memory confided to me a year later? When he actually spoke the words, with conviction, "This happened to me" in the therapist's office? Or years later, after the biggest rush of specific vivid details? Or most recently, on the night I made those apple pies and drove him to the venue, when he remembered the details of his friend's rape?

"What and when?" asked the second lawyer, well versed in claims against the American Boychoir School. These questions also included an implied "how much?"

Personal injury lawyers often work for 30 percent of any damage award. Damages are generally connected to physical injuries, and with the modest symbolic goal of a full tuition refund for his parents and possibly uninsured healthcare costs, Trav's circumstance is in no way a big moneymaker. After taxes and expenses, any settlement might buy a decent car or a year at a good college. And, again, the American Boychoir School's insurance company, not the school itself, would address the details.

That is how "what, when, and how much" morph into a complex algorithm of "Is it really worth it?"

For that car or tuition payment, Trav would need to out other victims and lose all of his privacy while subjecting himself to a years-long period of intense scrutiny. Or, he could get nasty and request even more money, knowing that any increased amount would prolong the process. In exchange for any settlement, there would almost certainly be a requirement that he not disclose the terms or discuss his experience.

Trav's fear is that he might disappoint me by not wanting to pursue legal action. "I am worried you will think I am weak," he once said.

Then, in a reversal a day later, it was "Screw them."

The next day, back to "No." Then, again, it was "I have nothing to hide."

That is what it is like. Some days, it feels worth a fight. Some days, just getting through the day is what matters.

Right now, he has taken it off the table. Most victims do.

CHAPTER SIX
New Jersey, Redux

I wish I had good words to describe New Jersey's physical details, but from the van I was unable to see beyond grimy green highway signs. As I searched for any positive association, even the abundance of hot and chewy Auntie Anne's salt-covered pretzels at nearly every turnpike rest area could not diminish the spaces' overwhelming toilet scent.

In the weeks before this trip, we had learned about a new movie in production. The early press publicized that the feel-good family film was about a young boy overcoming challenges through his involvement in a fictitious boy choir academy.

Trav tried not to think about it, and I tried not to bring it up on the trip.

If this portion of the story reads angry, it is because I am angry. For a partner, it is impossible to squelch that emotion entirely. Anger is real, and it can be all-consuming.

———

Initially, like many victims, Trav wanted an expression of regret. Acknowledgment, feeling heard by those responsible, and some version of "I am sorry this happened to you" are what many victims crave.

An apology was something tangible I could request without legal representation, and for me as a partner it felt like action, so, rejecting the legal process in favor of something more personal, I scanned the American Boychoir School's website. According to a 2002 *New York Times* article,[3] alumni from as late as the 1990s estimated that one in five students were molested, and with that statistic in mind, I studied the school's online photographs with a mathematician's eye, wondering who else in the alumni lineup might have been hurt.

There were no resources listed on the school's website, but in an upsetting discovery, Trav's little-boy face appeared in a promotional alumni lineup photo, his red hair distinct in the group of white robes. On the same page was a request for donations, and I let that sink in.

My husband's boyhood face was positioned on the alumni page, hustling for cash to support the school, and I wanted to smash the screen.

———

"Walk in love," Trav often advises, "not in anger or fear."

For many boys, maybe even *most* boys, the American Boychoir School experience was a positive one, so I sent a note to the school's acting

3 Schemo, Diana Jean. *"Years of Sex Abuse Described at Choir School in New Jersey."* THE NEW YORK TIMES, *April 16, 2002.*

representative. It was a simple and polite note that introduced myself and requested a conversation.

When I received no response, I sent a follow-up, and then made a third attempt. At the time of our road trip, I was still smarting from the lack of contact.

————

When we returned from the road trip, six months after the initial communication with the school, the acting representative agreed to talk. The man's telephone voice, soft and friendly, disarmed me. His tone sounded kind, and the kindness disarmed me, too. He made small talk, and I got the sense that if I met him at a company picnic or colleague's wedding reception, I might enjoy learning more about his life.

When our conversation moved toward Trav, I had three goals.

First, I asked him to remove Trav's photo from the alumni solicitation website page. Trav's photo, even in a group of other boys, placed alongside fund-raising requests felt almost criminal.

He agreed to this without hesitation, and the photo was gone the next morning.

"Excellent," I said, hoping my voice sounded as rational as his.

Second, I requested a tuition refund for Trav's parents, in 1988–1990 dollars. Trav's father, a middle school teacher, and his mother, a part-time hairstylist and homemaker, borrowed money to send their son to this school. Given Trav's negative experience, a tuition refund would demonstrate a symbolic good-faith effort to make amends.

Surprisingly, the acting representative agreed to consider the option, but he emphasized the organization's current precarious financial state.

He spent a great deal of time detailing the school's shaky finances. When he finished, I noted the equally overwhelming financial realities of victims.

I did not mention my review of the school's most recently reported federal income tax return, which listed more than eight million dollars in assets and six-figure salaries[4] for its administrators.

———

Still, our voices were calm. I said I understood, and I did. Nonprofit management can be daunting, and the prospect of managing a school beset with a reputation for childhood sexual abuse is, in many ways, an administrative nightmare.

He promised to look into the process of obtaining a tuition refund without a lawsuit, and while he never did call back, that was not the most disappointing aspect of the conversation.

The most disappointing aspect of the conversation was my third request, because this particular request cost no money at all. I asked the acting representative to make available, via a link on the school's website, a short list of resources for alumni who were sexually abused while in the school's care. I mentioned the organizations Male Survivor, 1in6, and Rape, Abuse and Incest National Network (RAINN).

He explained that his institutional priority is keeping the *current* students safe. He talked a great deal about this responsibility for providing safety, and although I had not asked, he assured me of the existing standards, policies, and protocols.

4 *Fiscal Year 2013 IRS Form 990.*

However, as recently as 2014, a former American Boychoir School dean was arrested for first-degree aggravated sexual assault against an eleven-year-old New Jersey boy.[5] When I asked about this arrest, the acting representative explained that the former employee's tenure was not recent and no reports were ever made of this man abusing boys while he worked at the school.

The silence hung between us in a situational irony that would have been comedic had the representative noticed.

When I asked if the school was dealing with any current sexual abuse allegations, he paused and told me he could not discuss details.

The conversation shifted to the upcoming film, and at that point my mind turned numb. I was prepared for resistance, disbelief, and possible hostility, but I had not prepared for this man accepting Trav's experience as true and then pivoting to a discussion of a Hollywood production with such glee and pride.

I remember mouthing, "Wow."

As if on cue, he told me his own son was an alumnus, and he shared my concerns. Then he listed the most tired of all the narratives. He told me the school was safe because he would never let his own son attend a dangerous environment.

"I said that if anyone hurt my son, I'd kill them."

I sighed.

This was when my "wow" turned into a stifled scream.

———

5 *"Former American Boychoir School Dean Arrested in Alleged Sexual Assault of New Jersey Boy,"* NEW YORK DAILY NEWS, *February 5, 2014.*

His response, however infuriating, is common. People often say some version of "If that happened to my boy, I'd kill the sonuvabitch." I understand the intention because I, too, reach for scraps of anything, including misinformed bravado, that might better the situation.

"Really?" I answer, feeling antagonistic. "How? Poison? A brick to the head? A gunshot?"

"Well," they say, in the usual response. "I'd sure sue the hell out of them."

These statements set my jaw hard.

"No," I answer, "you'd *want* to do those things."

Declarations that prison time would be well spent are easy, glib observations to make from a distance in hypothetical terms. The reality is much more complex; posturing and abstract ideas of vigilante justice are uninformed and unhelpful.

"With a brick to the head?" I wanted to ask that acting representative. "Or a gun?"

CHAPTER SEVEN
No Escape from New Jersey

I f the American Boychoir School's myopic approach was limited and restricted to a single individual acting as an interim representative, I could better understand, but these attitudes extend well beyond a single person, and cultural entrenchment is harder to address. Cultural entrenchment extends beyond a single school, and it affects any organization dealing with repercussions of child sexual abuse.

Alumni, students, faculty, constituents, and administrators must believe in the value of institutions facing child sex abuse allegations because to shift that perspective—however slightly or with compassion— means a shift in responsibility. That shift requires revising not just institutional policies, but institutional *philosophies*.

It is much easier to dismiss sex abuse as experimentation among peers or an anomaly limited to a few deviant adults, and this dismissive mentality or "us versus them" perspective leaves no room for broader cultural constructions or, most importantly, the victim's experience.

For instance, the mother of an American Boychoir School student sent me a note. She had read my published essays about the abuse Trav endured while attending the school, and she opened with an attempt at compassion.

"I am sorry this happened to your husband," she wrote to me, never, I noted again, doubting the accuracy of Trav's account. Instead of stopping with that concern, however, she immediately added a series of familiar conjunctions.

But it happened so long ago. But so few boys were molested. But the school is a much better place now. But there are policies. Those "buts" skipped over the victims so quickly, I am not sure she noticed. She called my portrayal of the school unfair and explained that her son's experience had been only positive. Her message—another script heard regularly by victims—was clear: Stop talking about it. Move on. Why spoil it for the rest of the boys?

"I am glad her son was not molested and raped," Trav told me when I shared her words. "Some of my friends and I were."

He continued, "Both things are true, and my experiences are no less important than her son's."

Now, in the midst of a massive fund-raising push (as of this book's writing), among the school's biggest arguments for continued support is nostalgia—that we, as a community, should not forget the school's impact and significance. And all those beautiful young voices.

But this is exactly what the school asks of its victims: Forget. Go away. Your once-heralded voice is no longer important.

This approach shuts down a conversation.

The mother extolled the school's positive impact and attached a photo of her smiling son as proof. She closed by inviting my family to attend the school's holiday concert as her guest.

My response, a sharply worded and unkind email, requested that she read her words aloud, and then continue reading them aloud until the cruelty and stupidity of those words set in. Choral music is a trigger that could easily send Trav into a funk that might take a week to emerge from, and the prospect of *literally* applauding the organization while sitting powerless in the audience would reinforce the memory of every time Trav was forced to smile and perform as a boy.

When I read her words to Trav's dad, his response was even more direct. "Is she kidding?"

Her note was not malicious, but it was thoughtless and unintentionally cruel. Like the acting school representative who spoke with me, this mother believed the school's messaging. To think otherwise would shake her foundation as a parent. Like that administrator, she had to believe her son was protected and her family immune.

I also noted in my response that Trav began drinking coffee at age eleven, so he could remain alert and vigilant at night.

"Does your son," I asked for a comparative reference, "drink coffee for this reason?"

As more and more institutions confront the unenviable task of responding to newly surfaced childhood sexual abuse allegations, there is much to be learned. For decades, the American Boychoir School, and others like it, have prioritized protecting the institution over caring for survivors of abuse perpetrated within the institution. Until that perspective shifts, I suspect this reputation for the child sexual abuse itself—*as opposed to how the victims were treated*—will persist.

These are the thoughts that occupied my mind in the last few moments of the van's hurried push toward the New Jersey border. My shoulders had tensed up, too, and the paper cup held in my hand since Maine was now a crumpled ball of damp cardboard.

Timelines for institutional atonement are complex, but I imagine the levels of possible healing would be great if the American Boychoir School officials (and others in charge at other institutions) changed the narrative and approached accusations of sex abuse from an initial position of compassion, with a simple "How can we help?"

Trav's suggestions would be direct. First, accept institutional responsibility. Next, provide a clear path for victims to access resources. Finally, be an innovative, collaborative voice in the conversation.

Or, if that feels too big and weighty a job to tackle, he would suggest starting with punctuation basics. Instead of compound sentences and conjunctions, use simple sentences. No more "I am sorry this happened, but . . ."

"I am sorry this happened." Period.

Anything else is the same old message.

CHAPTER EIGHT
Diner Pie

The sun set during the cross from New Jersey into Pennsylvania, and although the view of the road was dark, the space in the van felt measurably lighter. Trav turned down the radio and asked if I was hungry. Fresh air felt like a good goal, and the prospect of a leg stretch and some food felt even better.

Diners have a special significance for us because in addition to sharing diner pie on our first date, Trav and I believe "Breakfast served all day" is among the best sentences ever written. Eggs and toast, both inexpensive, offer a variety of choice—raisin or whole wheat with scrambled, over hard, or sunny-side up. "Whiskey toast," shorthand for rye, makes us both smile. There is something real, authentic, and brave about facing a cup of cheap coffee. It lacks pretense. Add an original diner car, and the elements of nostalgia increase. The chrome, the wood, and the padded bar stools firmly bolted to the floor create a beauty that is accessible, interesting, and secure.

One goal not reached on this trip was a visit to Providence's Johnson & Wales Culinary Arts Museum. Providence is where diners are reputed to have begun visiting Walter Scott's horse-drawn "Night Lunch Wagon" in 1872. Opening after traditional eateries closed, Scott offered hot and inexpensive food to late-shift workers, including those in the newspaper and theater professions.

A long history of cheap dates for the artistic crew, I thought.

"Diner-like" is fine, too, and to this end we chose a smoky, wood-paneled Pennsylvania truck stop for our first road trip supper and were seated by a server with faded and blurry indigo wrist tattoos. The table card advertised ninety-nine-cent tacos on Mondays, and Trav questioned the wisdom of truck stop taco night while Gloria Jones's original 1965 recording of "Tainted Love" played on the radio and I unfolded the cheap tin fork and knife wrapped tightly in a white paper napkin.

When I noted the music, Trav's humor turned base.

"You said ''taint.'"

I earned a terminal degree in writing and literature, but I still giggled.

Trav ordered eggs poached hard, and I reassured the server that yes, he really does love them cooked tough like rubber balls. It was an affirmation I had repeated at many different breakfast tables as part of the strange intimacy of knowing precisely how a spouse prefers to eat eggs.

In home-style restaurants, I have noticed servers are more likely to use "you" instead of "the." I mentioned as much when our own tattooed server stepped out of earshot with the menus tucked under her arm.

"How would you like *your* eggs?" is different from "How would you like *the* eggs?"

It might be a regional shift, but I suspect workers are smart to do this. It gives patrons a millisecond of power and importance. "Your eggs" makes a personal connection that "the eggs" lacks.

I noted the same for patrons. "I will take poached eggs" is more power-loaded than "May I please have poached eggs?" A weird cultural tic, I use it to separate the entitled from the considerate.

"You might be reading too much into it," Trav said when our food arrived, having listened to me talk about the importance of grammar and specific modifiers, the idiocy of *utilize,* and skin-grating mixed metaphors, for fifteen solid minutes.

He cut into his egg, cooked hard and rubbery as requested, with a fork.

The coffee's caffeine had kicked in, and just when I was about to begin a new declaration about the dumbing down of American culture, he set his fork onto his plate and squeezed my hand in a rare, spontaneous physical gesture.

"I am really glad we're doing this trip," he said.

And then: "You have eccentricities, too." Seeing my face register a level of hurt, Trav quickly softened the assessment and squeezed my hand again. "But I love your nerd brain so fucking much."

Love is patient, I remembered from the morning's Massachusetts billboard, thinking about the importance of semantics while still holding hands over our plates, aware that love suffers long—in both directions.

CHAPTER NINE
Capital Affair

After paying the bill, we decided to circumvent Washington, DC, and head south down the western spine of Virginia. After New Jersey, the District seemed too loaded, and neither of us felt up to tackling those memories outside the space we had created in the van.

Although we skipped DC, Trav and I talked about how we had met there as adults. With several hours of driving ahead of us, music playing low, and the heater blowing, I slipped my feet from my boots and tucked my knees onto the seat.

———

This story gets brought out, dusted off, and retold every year on our anniversary, and it has taken on a sparkling and mythical quality. *How did two people who grew up on the same street in Houlton, Maine, not meet until they were adults living in Washington, DC?*

I tell the story so often it has become a fan favorite.

"I brought him home with me, and he just never left" makes audiences laugh.

I share the bit about the black dress I bought, the party at the Bolling Air Force Base Officers Club where Trav and I were both working that night—he as Air Force entertainment, me to pick up a donation for a homeless services provider. I talk about watching the singer and thinking, "Wow, that looks like Tim and Dorene Humphrey's kid."

When I speak publicly, I note our age difference. Though it's negligible now, Trav returned from the American Boychoir School as an eighth grader while I counted down time as a graduating senior. I add that I used to babysit his classmates.

"Everyone," I say with a wink when I speak in public, "should date a twenty-three-year-old Airman."

I do not often share the bigger, broader details because it reveals a vulnerability that makes me uncomfortable. When Trav picked me up for our first date, he arrived at my Brookland neighborhood door holding a large bouquet of white Shasta daisies.

It was a long-running belief that I would recognize the man meant for me if he brought daisies instead of roses, and it was an indicator I had held fast to, eschewing the affections of many men who sent lovely rose-based arrangements. For me, roses read too traditional, too boring, and lacking imagination. Daisies symbolized originality, simplicity, a bigger truth, and recognition.

Trav's daisies unsettled me.

I thanked him, unwrapped the brown florist paper, and dusted an empty vase while he stood in the kitchen doorway. "If this works out,"

I said, snipping stems into the sink, "I will have a very funny story to tell you."

His oversized green Dodge pickup truck, better suited to our hometown's rutted, muddy farm roads than the uniform urban District streets, also unsettled me. His steady eye contact unsettled me, too.

––––––

We walked through the National Mall monuments. Lit up at night is my favorite way to experience them. Powerful in the sun, the behemoth Korean War Memorial soldiers look supernatural in the darkness. The Vietnam Veterans Memorial, always a shadowy presence, took on a greater significance when Trav stopped to point out a particular name etched into the smooth and polished black sheets of Bangalore granite.

"This man was my cousin," he said, touching the letters. I wanted to know more about this cousin, but we walked in silence, only breaking that heavy emotional space when we reached the steps of the Lincoln Memorial where we sat upon the same cool Georgia marble space from which Marian Anderson and Martin Luther King, Jr., had so famously projected their voices.

Trav and I talked until well past midnight on that humid May night while admiring the red lights at the top of the Washington Monument, as well as the glow of the obelisk in the water of the long, rectangular reflecting pool. I quoted a line from the Lincoln Memorial inscription: "In this temple as in the hearts of the people," and realized I had never before seen a man's eyes with Trav's peculiar, intense shade of blue.

Trav suggested late-night pie, and I agreed.

"I know this great place," he said, and we talked for three more hours across a table under the bright lights at Bob and Edith's twenty-four-hour Arlington diner. In the yellow booth, Trav ate his pie with enthusiasm, pausing only to lean over the table when I shared private life details that my closest friends still do not know. He nodded at each revelation. We skipped over superficial topics: books, music, religion, and politics, and it caught me off guard to hear the words that came from my mouth.

Childhood hurts, family drama, recent heartbreaks—Trav learned about my anxiety issues that first night, and I detailed a long list of experiences that had caused me fear and shame. As a naturally reserved person whose first impression is often described as both cold and conceited, I was surprised by my vulnerability in his presence.

Under those harsh diner lights, I laid out all my honest, emotional cards. I spoke about what I wanted and what I could offer. Rather than feel spooked or uncomfortable, Trav became more interested. He asked questions, and he listened to my responses.

———

In the van, we talked about that first date at Bob and Edith's Diner, and Trav recalled that the next morning he had written in his journal, "I met the woman I will marry."

Trav affirmed this as we drove along the dark highway.

"I just knew," he said.

When I agreed that I too knew immediately that Trav was the man for me, he called bullshit.

"Bullshit," Trav actually said, turning his eyes momentarily from the road to me in the passenger seat. "Bullshit," he repeated, laughing even harder. "When I asked you to marry me, you just said yes because you got embarrassed and didn't know what else to say."

He paused. "You figured you'd just get right with it in time."

He is probably correct.

I was drowning when I moved to Washington, DC. After I returned from a two-year, post-college AmeriCorps stint and an additional year working for a South Carolina homeless shelter, the plan was graduate school. Law or public policy; I had yet to decide. An aunt and uncle opened their Maine home to me, and for a year I hunkered down in their guest room.

It was a hard year. After a humiliating interview for a strip club position and a miserable summer job hustling beer and pulled pork at a barbecue joint, I took the first legitimate-sounding gig: grant writing.

Crippled with anxiety, I also lost thirty pounds. When I sat on the rocks at Fort Williams Park on Saturdays and watched the sky over the ocean change from intense summer blue to a more muted shade of winter gray, I often imagined the sensation of walking into those freezing wild waves and inhaling the salt water until the throbbing in my head finally ceased.

———

In the midst of this funk, an AmeriCorps buddy suggested I move to Washington, DC, to live as one of six roommates in a rambling neighborhood group house, and I said yes. My prior DC experience was limited to a short volunteer project at an inner-city elder care facility from where, almost every day at lunch, I walked to a corner café that sold hot tomato Florentine soup. I enjoyed that soup very much, and it was, I thought, a reasonable endorsement of the city.

Since this was before the Internet, cell phones, and global positioning systems, I found three nice-sounding jobs from a hard copy of the *Washington Post* and folded three resumes into envelopes. Three interviews and three offers later, I packed my little Mitsubishi truck and navigated around DC's Outer Loop by flipping through the highlighted pages of an old AAA TripTik.

To combat loneliness and limited resources in a new city, I explored the different neighborhoods, unwrapping homemade sandwiches at the marble Dupont Circle fountain and sampling discount California rolls while people-watching at Union Station. I read racy escort advertisements in the back of the *Washington City Paper* on the Metro's Red Line train, recognizing innuendo but not quite understanding the exact job description. I drank wine and lattes at a combined coffeehouse and lounge space in Adams Morgan, sinking into the venue's big purple velvet chairs.

Two weeks before I met Trav, I showed up at a personal ad brunch date wearing denim overalls, strung out from the tabs of Ecstasy I had swallowed while dancing the night before, babbling incoherent nonsense to a man whose name I cannot remember.

With pupils still dilated when I returned to my room, I wrapped a blanket around my shoulders and decided to change my perspective. Rather than continue to seek men according to physical type—tall, lanky, aloof, academic, or emotionally unavailable—I vowed to prioritize conversation, kindness, and humor. That same week, I also bought a fancy black dress for no real reason other than I liked it.

I walked the length of Georgetown's tony M Street twice, window-shopping and lonely. The dress, knee length and well constructed, graced a mannequin near the shop's front door, and in the dressing room it felt both sexy and professional on my body. The dress cost more than I could comfortably spend, but when I tried it on, it seemed like an investment and an adult purchase.

This dress hung on an old heating pipe that served as my closet until I agreed to cover an event for a coworker as a goodwill gesture. I do not remember if this coworker was sick or overloaded, but I do remember thinking that if the event ran late, it would excuse any next-day tardiness.

So, despite a cold and dreary May rainstorm, I found fake pearl earrings, applied makeup, buckled shoes, packed a tote bag with agency brochures, and wore the fancy black dress to a party at Bolling Air Force Base. I checked in at the security gate and dodged raindrops in the officer's club parking lot, thinking a raincoat might have been a smarter purchase.

With damp hair, I studied the lobby artwork while uniformed personnel clustered together in small groups, waiting for the banquet room doors to open. When dinner was called, I sat with the guest of honor at a table full of conservative, high-ranking male officers and their modestly dressed wives. A white lace cloth covered the table, and a baby shrimp fell from my salad fork and lodged into the open eyelet space of the lace, causing me a small panic when I tried to remove the shrimp unnoticed.

There was a presentation and then applause, and I accepted an enlarged check on behalf of the charity where I worked. I smiled for the photograph and thanked the assembled crowd with the short, two-minute version of my stock speech.

Then it got weird.

People raised in small towns with family names that extend back for centuries learn to spot certain genetic traits. A particular nose, build, or gait can predict family relations with a high level of precision, so during the musical entertainment I watched the singer wearing boots and a cowboy hat and instinctively thought, *Wow, that looks like a Humphrey*.

The singer's coloring matched the redheaded boy I remembered pedaling his bicycle along our shared hometown street. His nose and big, toothy smile were clear traits from his mom's side, and his general build and stance mimicked his father's with uncanny similarity. While Trav performed that night, I thought of when his mother hand-delivered a high school graduation gift to me, her neighbor. Wrapped in lavender paper and tied with a ribbon, it was an address book I still kept in my drawer.

The image I carried of Trav, thirteen, riding his bicycle in a woven anorak while I sped by him smoking a cigarette in my first car, did not match the grown, attractive singer onstage at the party. I had babysat Trav's peers, but like the rest of our community back then, I had zero awareness of what Trav had survived.

Before meeting Trav, I was also unaware of the United States Air Force Band. I was unaware the United States government is perhaps the largest single employer of artists, and each branch of the military—Air Force, Marines, Army, Coast Guard, and Navy—operates a band unit for morale and promotional purposes. I learned that under the band unit umbrella exist several, smaller ensemble bands, among them a string ensemble, a rock-and-roll band, and a show tunes-style performance band.

According to the party's program of events, Travis James Humphrey was the lead vocalist for the country-and-western group Silver Wings.

Trav was known in our hometown for his vocal talent, and he was featured often in the community newspaper.

Oh yeah, I thought, vaguely recalling a notice about him joining the Air Force.

The officers at the table, imposing men with sharp features, turned giggly when I made the connection, and they obliged my request for an introduction. After the event a colonel hopped up, and two minutes later Trav stood by our table.

"What are the odds?" the colonel asked as he helped his wife with her sweater.

By that point the party was dispersing, and it was just Trav and me standing in the nearly empty function room.

I want to say the connection was instant, but my mind was still processing the difference between the boy on his bicycle and the attractive man standing in front of me. I wrote my telephone number on one of the brochures, and he carried the oversized foam-board check to the parking lot for me.

"You drive a truck, too?" Trav asked, touching the toolbox mounted on my little Mitsubishi.

"Of course," I responded.

When I hugged him good-bye, the rain had stopped. If the energy was nondescript earlier in the day, it was positively charged on the drive across the District that night. The lampposts reflected light up from the still-wet streets when I parked my truck against the curb. I unzipped my black dress and hung it back up on the pipe. I went to sleep in my cheap earrings, face unwashed, and a feeling in my bones that something wonderful was about to happen.

CHAPTER TEN
Working Musician

"How do you do it?" I asked Trav about his musical talent during the long stretch of Virginia's Highway 81 on the way to Tennessee. It was the morning of our second day on the road, and since we planned to hit Nashville later that night, I wore cowboy boots stitched with bright orange flowers.

"Give me an example," he requested, so I described the weekend he was booked to perform a wedding, and he spent the morning of the ceremony strumming chords on his guitar. The bride had requested a dozen special songs, and four hours before guests were scheduled to arrive, Trav had just sat down to learn them all.

"I don't know," he said with a shrug, looking over his shoulder to switch lanes. "I just do."

Blessed with a high baritone and a functional 2.5-octave range that includes near-perfect relative pitch, Trav sings a dirge as easily as a lullaby.

While he barely reads traditional sheet music, Trav hears a song once or twice, notes the keys, and replicates it immediately.

He moves between Otis Redding and Katy Perry covers at his house gigs and wows crowds with original material on big stages; and his rendition of "What Child Is This?" has become a tradition at Christmas Eve services in our hometown. When he sings "Georgia on My Mind," I am convinced Hoagy Carmichael and Stuart Gorrell wrote the song especially for Travis James Humphrey.

Since he first picked up an instrument at age four, people have recognized his talent. There was something inherently charming and engaging about a big-cheeked little boy singing rock-and-roll standards.

It made sense that at age ten, after watching a traveling performance by the American Boychoir at the local high school, Trav would audition for a spot at that prestigious vocal academy. He impressed the selection committee with a rendition of Chuck Berry's "Johnny B. Goode," and his performance might have been a shock to a set of choral experts more accustomed to sixteenth-century madrigals.

Upon his acceptance to this school that accommodated grades four through eight, Trav's parents signed the contracts, purchased his navy-blue peacoat, and placed him on a plane. In the pre-Internet age, they were never informed of any sexual abuse allegations at the school, and they trusted the school's representatives.

They had no reason not to.

The American Boychoir School seemed like the opportunity of a lifetime. As parents, they intended to nurture and develop their son's talent. Trav, too, was excited to learn music in a novel manner, travel throughout the world, and meet new friends.

Upon his graduation from the American Boychoir School, Trav continued to make music in Aroostook County honky-tonks and wedding reception halls. In addition to his job as a teacher, Trav's dad owns a small musical instrument shop and hires himself out as an entertainer. As an adolescent, Trav played guitar and provided vocal support as his father taught him the trade of a working musician.

There are photos of Trav performing in high school competitions, grainy VHS tapes of songs in church, and at least fifty brides who exchanged rings or slow danced to the accompaniment of Trav's teenage voice.

With his innate vocal talent, capacity to learn music by ear, and ability to play any stringed instrument, Trav was recruited by the United States Air Force Band while still attending high school.

———

After two weeks of May dating, we decided to move in together when my lease arrangement ended. Trav was midway through a second enlistment, and our first shared space was a tiny cinder block Shirlington studio. We used camp chairs as furniture, and at one point our bed was a mattress made up on the floor. Trav nailed up unframed posters to decorate the wall.

The brown plastic industrial tarp he used to block all window light, I insisted, had to go.

At the time, neither of us recognized the significance of that tarp.

He had duct-taped the tarp over the single window that ran the length of the studio space, reinforcing the edges to shut out any possibility of sunlight.

"It helps me sleep," he said, but the creep factor of zero light through the duct-taped tarp felt too high for me. Cocking my head and squinting my eyes did little to improve the tarp's appearance.

I offered heavy curtains as a compromise. I would later learn that many victims prefer total light or total darkness to feel safe enough to sleep.

Fronting an Air Force ensemble band was a good job, but it stifled Trav, and I watched two different personalities emerge. Onstage, Trav was lively, gregarious, and fun. He shook his ass, learned contemporary songs, and flirted with sassy elderly ladies in the audience.

In our little apartment, he hid under a blanket on the couch.

After watching his sunny stage presence lie dormant under that blanket for a year, I suggested Trav visit the base clinic, and he received a ten-question checklist.

"You're fine," the clinician said, and sent Trav back to our couch.

It had taken so much effort for Trav to make that first clinician appointment, and when his symptoms were evaluated in a single minute and dismissed as inconsequential, it reinforced all the negative messaging that he should get over it because whatever "it" was, it would pass.

Except it did not pass. In fact, his funk worsened.

That is when he agreed to see a private physician. This physician sat down, took time with him, established a family history, and listened carefully to his words. Since one particular antidepressant had worked for a family member, the physician asked if he would like to try it.

In a week Trav was off the couch, and with that small dose of antidepressant, information began to slip out.

"I can't remember all the details, but I have this feeling," he said about his time as a choirboy, and I held his hand as the night terrors, hypervigilance, and claustrophobia began to make sense. It was a brave moment of trust that shifted the trajectory of our partnership.

"I believe you," I said. "Tell me more if you want to."

"This feeling," we would later learn, is a classic textbook process for how adult victims of childhood sexual abuse begin to recall and understand their experiences. After they stuff details away in an effort to survive, these details often emerge slowly, much later, in fragments and via a series of felt senses.

When people asked about Trav's experience in the military, I described the Garth Brooks-style shirts, the cowboy hat and boots, the string tie, and the huge Air Force belt buckle. I mentioned his capacity as an emergency medical technician, too. When he was promoted to master sergeant, I beamed.

"My husband is basically the president's house band," I bragged.

All these aspects of our life were accurate, but I have learned that many, often conflicting things can be true simultaneously.

For years, nobody knew about Trav's dark parts.

———

As Trav recalled more details, nights got harder. The job, too, got weirder.

For one presidential inauguration parade, Trav was instructed to arrive before sunrise, handed a tuba, and expected to carry the instrument both in the parade's lead-up formation and throughout its duration. Snow, sleet, and freezing rain fell all day, and Trav shivered in his uniform.

"Why a tuba?" I asked when he arrived, soaking wet, at the apartment. While gifted with stringed instruments, Trav had never played the wind variety, and certainly not with expertise as part of the larger concert band.

"They wanted to bulk up the parade presence, and I guess I was strong enough to hold the heaviest instrument for eight hours."

The ridiculousness was not lost on either of us.

———

While I thrived with our weekend trips to the underground intricacies of Luray Caverns, the engineering ingenuity at Thomas Jefferson's Monticello, and the Maine-like blue ocean coast of Maryland's Eastern Shore, Trav grew more withdrawn. Not even the recording process for his first solo album, *Yellow Cat Blues,* boosted his spirits for any length of time.

We had also experienced the September 11 Pentagon crash less than two miles from our apartment building. A disgruntled scientist killed five people and injured seventeen others by sending anthrax via the local post office. Thirteen random people were shot during the many weeks of the Beltway sniper attacks, and one of those women was killed beside her husband in the same Falls Church Home Depot parking lot where I had bought kitchen shelving on the weekend prior to her death.

During the sniper attacks, Trav and I shifted away from our usual seats in the local bagel shop's front windows to a darker corner table, and it occurred to us that DC was not a long-term solution. Neither of us wanted to choose bagel shop seating based on fear of random death.

During this external chaos and in the midst of Trav's depression, when the institutionalized lifestyle of the Air Force reflected that of the American Boychoir School—take orders, do not complain, smile, sing, perform for the crowd even when the situation feels very, very wrong—became too much, Trav inched his way back toward the couch and blankets.

Trav's dosage increased, and we signed an apartment lease in Maine. "But you've got eight years in," people criticized.

We were called stupid and shortsighted and accused of wasting good careers, but if we stayed, I was certain Trav would put a bullet into his head. I said, "Let's go home," because I did not know what else to do.

With no jobs and $10,000 in our checking account, we drove straight through a March night. By then we had acquired two cats, and they yowled for the entire trip.

We made it to the new apartment in the darkest hours, and when the sun eventually filtered through our bare bedroom window, the air mattress had deflated, and we woke on the hardwood floor, shivering under our winter jackets. The cats hid high up on the strange new pantry shelves, and neither Trav nor I could figure out the heating system.

"What have we done?" I wondered aloud, rubbing my arms for warmth, watching snow begin to fall, and hoping the Amato's Sandwich Shop across the street sold coffee.

This move to Maine began Trav's career as a working musician. More than a decade later, he has built up his business on his own terms, one small stage at a time. Music, for Trav, is a job. It is also his vocation and a means to a financial end. The American Boychoir School experience ensured that Trav would rarely expect artistic joy in the experience of making music.

"Man, what is he doing here?" is the most common question about Trav's talent. He hears this often from the small, makeshift corner stages at local dive joints, and the answer is that his business model is a little different. Rather than chase fame on the road, Trav built a rotation of regular house gigs in Maine.

"This way," I explain, "he earns a decent living, and he gets to sleep in his bed every night."

It is the simplest explanation.

Sometimes I say, "Oh, it is a long story."

Both are true.

Yes, Trav is a world-class musician. Trav once performed with Murali Coryell, son of blues guitarist Larry Coryell, as the opening act for B.B. King. He has opened for Ricky Skaggs. While fronting Silver Wings, he performed on *The Today Show,* at Constitution Hall, and on the steps of the Capitol. He also headlined Canada's East Coast Opry Show.

But as a general rule, he sings for lobstermen, laborers, carpenters, white-collar professionals, and tourists.

"I go where the sinners are," a young Latino priest once explained to me when I questioned the seeming incongruity of his love of salsa venues, and the adage applies to Trav as well.

Trav performs for the local, the lost, and the lonely. While he would love to work bigger stages, the price to get there is steep, and what I do not tell those wondering why Trav chooses happy-hour shows instead of the Nashville or Austin hustle is that on most days, despite the dancing and hilarious stage banter, it takes six prescription medicines and a strict and structured lifestyle regimen for my husband to function.

Trav is often called a musician's musician, and in addition to his regular shows he is often sought for studio session work. If Trav moved to Nashville or Austin, he would join thousands of aspirants, all with a degree of talent, in the push-and-shake process, performing for tips in a pickle jar and angling for work while trying to sell songs.

I imagined him walking from club to club, handing out a press kit that would be put in a drawer with all the other press kits. In the best-case scenario, he might establish himself as a local and get a regular gig. Maybe he would make friends with an industry professional looking to add talent to their songwriting roster. It took ten years to build his modestly profitable business in Maine, and we shied away from the prospect of pushing that reset button in a region where, in our experience, many artists spend time not developing their business acumen or mastering their talent, but, rather, hoping to be "discovered" by someone else.

Trav's existing national connections are limited to the point of near invisibility compared to the tight, solid, extended network of friends and family we have cultivated in Maine. In Maine, he performs five shows weekly for fans who know his name.

One newspaper reporter called Trav "the hardest-working musician in Maine," and those words did not describe Trav's hustling skills, but instead Trav's business model and priorities. "Mr. Integrity" is another moniker put on him, and if every person touched by Trav's integrity stood up to be counted, it would be a fierce, impenetrable circle.

In Maine, Trav makes a decent living by performing music. He performs songs people enjoy, charges a fair price, and drives home to me at night.

———

There is a family photo of baby Trav lying beside his father while his father plays a guitar. Baby Trav is reaching up for the strings, and his parents have long cited this image as the moment Trav fell in love with music.

I suspect one of the moments Trav fell in love with me was when I said that he interested me because of who he was as a person, not the music he makes.

"Music is who I am," he explained earnestly during our blushing, two-week courtship.

"No," I recall arguing, "music is something you do."

He looked at me with a crooked expression. It was the first time someone succinctly separated the two things.

This is when we talked about his musical identity. I enjoyed the music he made, but what interested me most were the books he read, how he spent his time, and the causes he cared about.

"I wouldn't care if you ever sang another song," I told him.

CHAPTER ELEVEN
Trigger Warning

The Nashville skyline appeared at dusk, and before finding our hotel we diverted across town and past the fancy Belle Meade mansions off Highway 100 for supper at the Loveless Café. Both of us avoid eating animals, but the Loveless Café's watermelon-glazed ribs would make even the most resolute vegetarian waver.

"Pork is the tastiest of all meats," Trav said as the scent of bacon wafted through the dining room. And then, even more thoughtfully, he added, "I have probably eaten more pigs than you." Trying to calculate the number of pigs consumed led to speculation that it would make more sense if, rather than eating an apple, it was killing an animal and discovering its tastiness that got Adam and Eve kicked out of Eden.

Watching the biscuit production behind the plate-glass window in the long-ago-converted motel complex is mesmerizing, and I doubt Lon and

Annie Loveless could have imagined the appeal of Annie's original biscuit recipe for this Maine couple. When we visit Nashville, it is generally our first stop, as it is for many tourists from many other states.

While the Loveless Café is in no way a locals-only joint, the cluttered and abundant arrangement of framed celebrity publicity shots testifies that locals—or, at least, the famous ones—do frequent the restaurant. That wall of photos reminds us, too, that the celebrities in those photos are actual, real performers who once sat at the same tables to eat biscuits.

That awareness is humbling. So often, it is easy to mythologize celebrity and its pursuit, and as Trav and I spread more butter and preserves on what felt like our millionth blissfully fluffy biscuit, we wondered why we had opted not to move to Nashville.

Then we remembered.

———

A few years prior, I had received a job offer just outside Nashville. In light of the opportunity, Trav thought he might try his luck in what many people consider the music industry big leagues. He had a loose session guitarist connection and an even looser songwriting connection.

Kid-free and restless, we thought, *Why not?*

We had lived in Maine for several years, and Trav's diagnoses finally felt manageable. Life had become even-keeled, and both of us liked the prospect of an adventure. Trav also felt the urge to stretch himself artistically.

In anticipation of this potential move, we visited a Nashville real estate agent's office. We explained that we were left-leaning people who desired a pedestrian-friendly location. This woman's tone, enthusiastic in our initial email communications, became even more so on the telephone. In person, she oozed hospitality, fussing over my hair and shoes. She shared the office space with a partner, and as she made a big, sweeping effort to learn about our situation, the partner quietly organized materials on his desk.

"So," she said, making intentional eye contact and nodding, "tell me more."

Our mortgage preapproval letter read extravagant, but even our much lower agreed-upon budget would buy us a solid middle-class house and offer her a nice commission. With our good credit and VA eligibility, options seemed plenty. I explained that school districts were less important to us, and we could risk an up-and-coming area. We wanted walkability, history, and proximity to a library, college, park, or downtown. No pre-planned developments, no nearby strip malls, and no cul-de-sacs.

"We have animals," I said, noting our desire for a small yard, "but we would consider the right townhouse situation."

The real estate agent kept nodding, and given our fluid timeline and lack of any contractual contingencies, we presented well.

"As a reference point," I continued, looking at Trav for affirmation, "we are pretty comfortable in the historically gay neighborhoods of major cities."

"So," I explained, "think about the Castro, the Village, and DC's Dupont Circle. Maybe we could start there, but in Nashville?"

Trav says I illustrated these statements by counting on my fingers and emphasizing as if I were teaching students from a lectern. This gesturing is a tic I rarely notice, but it annoys Trav when I lapse into "professor" mode, so I try to be conscious of my delivery.

This is when her nod ceased, mid-descent, and her little jaw hung loose.

Her coworker in the corner, silent until this moment, stopped his filing, whistled, and put his fingers into his ears for emphasis. At the whistle, I turned in his direction.

"La la la," he said, "I am gonna pretend I didn't hear that."

The real estate agent's shoulders straightened, but she resumed her affectations, this time much slower. Her voice lowered in tone and took on a slower cadence, too, as if I had transformed into a cognitively impaired toddler.

"This is the South," she said, still nodding. "And Nashville does not have a gay district."

She sifted through an inch-thick stack of home listings she had printed for us to consider. Crumpling all but two pages into the wastebasket, she stood up.

"Then you wouldn't like those." She pointed toward the papers in the bin. "Those are for *families*."

In the span of ten minutes, she had moved from charming to escorting us to the door. We stood in the empty parking lot with our two sheets of paper, wondering what had just happened.

"Well," Trav said, "that was a pretty big 'fuck off.'"

On our own, we drove by the first listing, a grimy tract house situated behind an overgrown lawn. A burnt-out car had been pushed to the side of the driveway, and, ever the optimist, Trav pointed out its Barack Obama bumper sticker.

"She didn't even know about your security protocols," I remarked, thinking not about our relatively short list of "must haves," but about all the criteria I had deliberately withheld because something as ordinary as home buying becomes heavily influenced by the childhood sexual abuse experience.

For Trav, the list is long.

In addition to our aesthetic distaste for cul-de-sacs, a real estate agent would need to cross off all homes with skylights. No walls of windows, no glass doors, a perimeter that is easily reinforced, potential for double or triple locks on exterior access points, wide distance between neighbors, privacy fencing, motion lights, at least two floors, and no established landscaping to inhibit visibility. Trav would have requested an open-concept floor plan, not for the versatility and airiness but for the clear and easily defensible sightlines.

———

The negative Nashville home-buying experience had happened many years ago, and during our current meal at the Loveless Café on our first night in Tennessee, we were hopeful and thought we might revisit the idea of a move. Stuffed full of turnip greens and feeling fine, we paid the bill and rolled ourselves back into the van, talking about all the ways we could make a relocation work. It was a dreamy headspace, and we brainstormed during the half-hour drive to the hotel.

Upon arrival, I knew we had made a terrible mistake.

The hotel, a midprice national brand, looked fine in its Internet photos. We had planned two nights—time for Parnassus Books, music at the Bluebird Café, and a trip to the Gruhn Guitars store.

The chlorine pool smell hit us hard when we entered the lobby, and the fluorescent lighting flickered unevenly. After the desk clerk presented the key card, we walked the length of the dark hallway with both recessed and protruding areas that cast long shadows.

Trav's frame tensed up.

The room door rattled open on weak hinges, and while many people check the comfort of hotel beds first, that ranks on the bottom of our list. The room, second floor as requested, was modest. Modest felt okay, but after touching the door's hinges, Trav walked to the windows. The window locks were loose, too.

His neck began to flush.

It was late. I was tired. While neither one of us was hungry, we had driven all day and both our backs ached.

Had I been traveling solo, I would have pulled the chain link across the latch and called it good, trusting the suburban neighborhood's well-lit safety. For Trav, no heavy chair in the room meant no way to brace the door. He can handle the standard double lock if there is a chair to improvise with. Without a chair or heavy desk to reinforce the door, the room was not an option.

I could tell he was trying to breathe through the details, and I sat on the edge of one of the beds.

Trav started to pace.

"I am sorry," he said.

"It's okay," I answered.

That is what the effects of sex abuse look like. It is not the heightened drama of inpatient hospitalization and a hand-wringing suicide watch, with atmospheric highs and subterranean lows. More often, sex abuse triggers mean little moments like last-minute hotel switches.

In that Nashville hotel room, I was still smarting from the last trigger moment. It was on my mind because we had had a month without a major incident, and a month felt like a big win.

———

The last incident happened when, upon marriage equality's legalization, two friends eloped, and a celebration was later hosted in their honor. I drove to this party alone with my scarf pulled tight against the December chill, because although Trav had planned to join, he experienced a last-minute episode after watching a television news segment of his former coworkers in the Air Force Band performing a choral version of "Jesu, Joy of Man's Desiring."

The segment was a holiday feature, and along with the sound of a beautiful piece of music, the camera panned across the straight-backed vocalists, the shiny euphoniums, and the string players, all crisp in their blue uniforms.

Trav's eyes turned wet when he saw the screen.

It was not the reaction I expected, and, snapping the television off, I moved toward him on reflex, thinking fast. Was it the choral music? The song itself? The holidays? The Air Force? There was a trigger somewhere in the mix, and I waited for him to catch a breath.

Like most of his triggers, it inspired self-loathing.

"If I hadn't been fucked up as a little kid, do you think I'd still be in the military?" he asked, and I struggled for an honest answer.

Probably, I thought, but I said, "Maybe."

I reminded him that if he had stayed, we would be breathing unhealthier air, we would hate the traffic, and we would have lessened our family connections.

I thought, but also did not say, that he would likely be dead.

Logically, he knows this. He also knows he is pushing middle age and feeling like he has missed opportunities. He wonders how his life might look if the daily struggle to manage symptoms did not exist.

That night at the celebration of our friends' marriage, I made his last-minute excuses, ate cake, and enjoyed the festive atmosphere, and I thought about Trav as Orion brightened the sky during my quiet drive home.

Again, pain for partners is rarely in moments of enormous crisis, but rather in the little moments of arriving solo, late, or not at all.

———

Together we rolled our luggage back through the Nashville hotel lobby, and I apologized to the front-desk clerk. It was a third-party reservation, so in the parking lot while I waited for Trav to move the van, I called to cancel the following nights. I calculated the financial loss, and I pulled up other last-minute hotel options.

Back in the van, we navigated our way to the opposite side of Nashville.

"I am sorry," Trav repeated, clearly ashamed.

"It's okay," I said again.

These were the only words we spoke, with the exception of the name of the new hotel and the directions.

This is our reality: pivoting in strange hotel rooms, apologizing to staff, and negotiating reservations after midnight when the details become too much to bear. In a strange way, the process is also empowering for Trav. As a grown man, he trusts his assessment powers, and if a situation feels wrong, he possesses the capacity to recognize and change it.

The new hotel, a behemoth in our price range only because of the last-minute need, fit our criteria. The lobby was enormous and bright, the security staff obvious, and the hallways wide with clear sightlines.

Trav loaded our bags into the new room, and this time his comportment was much more relaxed. Two secure locks on a heavy metal door with tight hinges, third floor, two beds, and a solid chair.

As Trav did his nightly preparations, I did mine. I removed my clothing, washed my face, turned back the bedcovers, sank into the mattress, and fell asleep within five minutes.

Trav walked the perimeter of the exterior, and then the interior, casing his surroundings. In the process, he met some bluegrass musicians in the hotel lounge. With every detail secure in his mind, he jammed with his new friends until the early-morning hours.

The next day, once again at the Loveless Café, we spread strawberry jam over more biscuits. As we sorted out how to spend the afternoon, triggers were still on our minds. With our coffee cups refilled and eating pace slowed down, Trav leaned back in his chair to stretch his arms.

"I cannot believe they are making a movie."

I chewed more biscuit.

"What's next?" he wondered aloud. "Penn State: The Musical?"

It made no sense to me either when I first read the details.

"Did anybody do an Internet search on the school's history?"

I had no answer.

If holiday choral music on the news and loose hotel room hinges set my husband's subconscious spinning, I imagined the effect of driving past the name of a movie in capital letters on theater marquees every night during the movie's run.

Later, I would write an essay. Then I would write personal notes to people affiliated with the film. I would receive a cease-and-desist letter from the film company's lawyers, and in response we would hire our own attorney. Despite early promotional photos, the film company denied association with any specific boy choir school.

———

When the movie was just an abstract concept at the Loveless Café table, it seemed far away and benign. Months later, when our Loveless Café biscuits were a vague memory and the film promotion began in earnest, Trav got mad.

Not just mad. One night Trav became pissed off in a manner I had never witnessed.

He read some early reviews and slammed our kitchen door.

I did my best feral-soothing voice, offering the now familiar "Look at Lawrence Lessig's public-facing career. He's not just known for the Boychoir—he's a kick-ass lawyer."

Lessig, the alumnus lawyer who, for years, stuck with a legal battle[6] to hold the school accountable for child sexual abuse, was a powerful and inspirational figure for Trav. "Boychoir is just one thing that happened in his life."

---

6 HARDWICKE V. AMERICAN BOYCHOIR SCHOOL. *Decided August 8, 2006.*

"Things," I reassured Trav, "are getting better."

I cited the Louis Freeh report[7] about the child sexual abuse scandal at Penn State and how the former FBI director, a respected man, delivered a professional version of "No fucking way should this have happened."

Even after reminding Trav of the men working hard to force a culture shift, and that he was so, so brave for choosing to live with this issue, that night there were only tears and rage.

———

Ultimately, rage can be a good thing.

Rage is often a man's reaction. No longer a scared little boy hiding in the woods or a hallway cabinet space, Trav has worked through a range of adult emotions, and rage was at the top of that night's list.

"FUCK them, Shonna," he hollered. "FUCK them because I cannot get away from this. Even if I try to put it behind me, it keeps presenting itself."

He took a breath, still pacing. "I've got a whole list of shitty choices. Every time I try to get past this, something else comes up. And now they are making a FUCKING MOVIE."

He kept going while I nodded.

"I tried to forget it, then I tried to deal with it."

He sat down at this point, and this is when the angry tears came. Then he stood up again.

"I gave up whiskey. I accepted some pretty fucking scary diagnoses. I exercise. I eat right. I see a therapist every two weeks. I let you write about this."

7 *"Special Investigative Counsel Report Regarding Actions of Penn State."*
   Freeh, Sporkin & Sullivan, July 12, 2012. Web. February 17, 2016.

Then more tears came. He slapped the arm of the couch.

"When does it fucking end?"

He held his head with his hands.

Then he looked at me in a way that leaves partners like me feeling useless and wholly inadequate. "What do I have to do?"

He repeated the question, slower. "What . . . do . . . I . . . have . . . to . . . do?"

I sat, useless, while he continued.

"So, now I can just shut up?" he said. "And let that movie come out while people who know I attended a school like that ask me about it every day?"

He wiped his eyes and nose, first with his sleeve and then with a tissue I handed him.

"They fucking made a fucking movie about this," he repeated, quieter.

"Fuck them," he said again, this time in a whisper.

By this time he had sat down, and I moved closer to rub his back.

He sighed. "I could sue the fuck out of the school for years of my life, and then be slapped with a 'Do not discuss' clause in exchange for some cash."

I nodded.

"Or, I can have you write more about it and keep the whole thing even more front and center."

Calmer now, he squeezed my hand.

"And maybe that is where it needs to be. Maybe I need to face this thing in the biggest way possible."

Trav paused, and I wiggled into the nook under his arm with my hand resting on his chest. We breathed together for a few minutes.

"I don't fucking know, Shonna," he finally whispered, which was good because I, too, had no answers. "They are all shitty choices."

"Yes," I said. He was correct.

"Not making a choice feels like the worst option," he said, and I agreed. "I can't ever get away from this."

———

During Trav's moment of rage, I spun my wedding ring with my thumb. It is a nervous habit, and when I am deep in thought or angry, I run my thumb along the little callus developed by this action.

The silver ring's interior is inscribed with the phrase "Tell Travis you love him." We bought the ring at a shopping mall, and the saleslady called to tell me the phrase was too long to fit on such a tiny piece of jewelry, so I agreed to a shorter sentence: "I love Travis."

When Trav picked up the ring, he was frustrated by the change. As a surprise, he took the ring to a different engraver who did his best to rub out the compromise inscription and replace it with the original.

Trav showed me the ring, apologetic for the scuffing in the background. The first inscription had been cut deep, and there was no way to remove all traces, but there were the new words, clearly visible. "Tell Travis you love him."

I do not mind the scuffed background. It is messy and it devalues the ring, but now the ring is unique, and those scars remind me of the words Trav spoke when he brought my wedding ring to me.

"I want you to have exactly what you want in this world."

———

I thought about this as I sat with Trav on the couch during the rage-filled night. Looking at my husband's blotchy and tired face, there was no way I could make his scars heal. There was no way I could make it right. There was no way I could reshape the experience of childhood sexual abuse into a quirky and unique feature, like the scuff marks underneath my wedding ring's inscription.

I, too, wanted him to have exactly what he wanted, but all I could do was spin my wedding ring aimlessly with my thumb. I put my head against his shoulder and said the only words that came to mind.

"I love you, Trav."

———

But during that breakfast at Nashville's Loveless Café, while chatting over the red-checked tablecloth between our coffee and next biscuit order, I spun my wedding ring and thought about its inscription, not because my husband was feeling rage, but because the tic had become habit.

That day, we were just talking hypotheticals. The movie was not real yet. It was just an abstract concept, but if the real triggers were any indication, it would be a miserable life during that movie's run.

CHAPTER TWELVE

Guitar Store Bunny Ranch

O n our Nashville agenda, very near the top of the list, was scouting the new location of Gruhn Guitars. Formerly situated on lower Broadway, Gruhn had moved to a neighborhood on 8th Avenue, not far from Interstate 65 and Wedgewood, and the new space was impressive. No longer crammed into a heavily trafficked tourist corner between Hatch Show Prints and a souvenir shop stuffed full of Confederate flag memorabilia, the layout was vast. Best of all, there was a dedicated parking lot, and I watched a happy Trav practically skip from the van to the door.

Highly polished wood floors mirrored the shine on the silver resonator guitars, and, attracted immediately to their sparkle, Trav dropped to a knee and inspected the instruments in reverent worship.

The salesman smiled a welcome, and I poked around the walls upon walls covered with stringed instruments, noting the subtle differences.

Thanks to Trav, I could distinguish a sunburst from a natural finish, and I could appreciate an intricate mother-of-pearl fret board inlay in the tiniest vine, fleur-de-lis, or bird form. Trav showed me how the finish cracks on the back of an old guitar are called checking, and rather than lowering the value, they can authenticate and help in dating or appraising an instrument.

"It's like his Bunny Ranch," I said to the salesman, who laughed at the reference.

"Oh, I have a story about that."

I wish I remembered the details of his Moonlite Bunny Ranch story, but at the exact moment the salesman began to speak, with Trav still strumming the chrome-shiny National guitar, I looked over the salesman's shoulder and saw musician Brian Setzer standing at the far counter, talking with another associate.

While the salesman told his story, I was confirming that, in fact, Brian Setzer stood thirty feet away from me. The surreal beauty of the moment washed over me.

I am standing in the Gruhn Guitars store, ten steps away from Brian Setzer, while Trav plays a National guitar and the salesman is telling me his Bunny Ranch story.

It felt like a Fellini-esque dream, and I thought, "This." This is what I wanted: more moments like this. Moments when my husband was engrossed in the experience of high-quality musical instruments, happier than I had seen him in months, and I was engrossed in the bizarre and completely random process of pretending not to notice the versatile and internationally regarded musician whose Stray Cats cassette had played on repeat in my teenage bedroom, while trying to focus on the details of the salesman's story about one of Nevada's most famous brothels.

At that moment, child sexual abuse was the furthest thing from my mind.

———

Trav bought a simple capo, used for raising the pitch on stringed instruments, as well as a single thirty-five-dollar Blue Chip guitar pick, sad that our financial situation prevented us from backing the van up to the door and loading in a brand-new guitar collection, or at least another instrument to add to his current collection.

"Our financial situation" is when the sex abuse experience often resurfaces.

In addition to the emotional costs, cash outlays are a reality for families dealing with the repercussions of childhood sexual abuse. Extra money is needed for alternative treatments and other uninsured expenses, and despite our earning decent wages, a new instrument was not an option on this trip.

———

"If I could go back," Trav's mom told me recently, "I would undo all of it."

I know she means it. What parent wouldn't?

A sentimentalist, Trav's mom saves ephemera. Newspaper clippings, photos, wedding programs, church bulletins, birth announcements, and special cards all mean a great deal to her.

She collects these ephemera with precision and loves to remember each carefully folded experience. She is thoughtful, and it was this thoughtfulness that had prompted her to hand me a large manila envelope during a visit home. Inside the envelope was a packet of letters from Trav's Boychoir days.

The content of those letters, written in a little boy's messy cursive over the span of thirty months, moved from initial excitement punctuated with double and triple exclamation marks to rote summaries of places visited and assignments completed. Trav shifted from describing internal emotions during the first few anticipatory weeks to a gradual reduction of those feelings over time, with the last letters containing nothing but dry physical landscape descriptions and lists of completed assignments.

The exception was a page of lyrics from a song he penned at age thirteen that describes his failure as a son.

In hindsight, it is easy to understand the shift.

The letters were difficult to read, but beneath those letters were the pieces that made the experience very, very real. Underneath the letters was a stack of canceled checks for uniform fees, parent association dues, and tuition payments. There were reimbursements for teacher supplies and a copy of the school contract. Those canceled checks and money orders were stacked as thick as my wrist.

"I don't think this is all of them," Trav's mom apologized, "but it was all I could find."

Added up, that small sample of canceled checks represented a full year of my father-in-law's northern Maine teacher's salary.

I wrapped my mind around that detail. Trav's parents borrowed and saved, and they spent at least a full year's income to enroll their son in a school meant to showcase and develop his musical talent.

Those first canceled checks just begin the cash tally. I can produce a file of receipts for a decade of copays, prescription costs, and out-of-pocket mental health treatment expenses.

Harder to quantify are the "what ifs?" Had Trav remained in the Air Force, his income would have been stable and substantial. He left with the rank of master sergeant, impressive for a then-twenty-five-year-old noncommissioned officer. That lost income is significant. The military pension? Even more so.

I believe victims who sue for damages are rarely motivated by greed or vengeance entirely; it is basic survival. The realities of childhood sexual abuse include the likelihood that Trav will need treatment for the rest of his life.

———

During our first years in Maine, we had no health insurance coverage. We blew through our $10,000 cash cushion and racked up twice that amount in credit card debt. I once held Trav while he hallucinated during the early-morning hours due to a particularly brutal medication shift, and amidst my eagerness for the drug's half-life to diminish in his body, I wondered how we would pay for any increased level of care. That rough night happened before the Affordable Care Act, and I found myself crying when a social worker explained over the phone that as a kid-free couple with incomes, we did not qualify for any type of assistance.

There is reluctance to put a price tag on damages, and the laws in many states provide for only some version of the "physical" damages suffered.

This is the part of the narrative where I imagine readers leaning in for details. How bad was it? For how long? How many employees committed those sex acts? What body parts were touched? Genitals? Mouths?

One or two indelible images might be effective, but when specific violations are placed on a list in order of perceived severity, the associated emotions for each act are *exactly the same* for victims: fear, shame, trauma, sadness, and grief.

There is no "molestation lite."

Let me repeat that phrase. There is no "molestation lite," and the process of placing a ranked dollar value on physical activity is a sick sort of math. It might work for a brothel, but it does not compute for child sexual abuse.

To think otherwise makes us both very angry. Yes, Trav knows that at least one American Boychoir School student's body likely required surgery to heal.

Is that, we wonder, *the level of detail necessary to be eligible for compensation?*

CHAPTER THIRTEEN
Heritage, Not Hate

During our days in Nashville, Trav and I visited Cooter's Place, a cluttered museum stuffed with dusty *Dukes of Hazzard* television show memorabilia and cutoff denim shorts strung on a clothesline. Its location was along the way to Parnassus Books, a shop on my priority list, so when we saw the iconic orange Dodge Charger emblazoned with the Confederate flag, we raced each other to say it first.

"Heritage," I blurted.

And then Trav nodded sagely. "Not hate."

While we appreciate that some people believe that maxim, the concept has turned into an inside joke, guaranteed to make us both laugh.

Cooter's Place reminded me of the International Cryptozoology Museum at home in Maine. Loren Coleman, among the world's foremost experts in the field of cryptozoology, built a dusty collection of items related to presumed mythological creatures including the yeti, Loch Ness Monster, Sasquatch, chupacabra, and the coelacanth.

Behind glass at both museums are toys, posters, and stacks of other vintage items.

For a birthday treat, I once arranged for a private tour of the International Cryptozoology Museum.

Trav and Loren Coleman discussed Jungian transference with agitated, animated tones, and that discussion happened not far from a hair-covered, life-sized Bigfoot model. When I tired of their banter, I admired the Bigfoot and then amused myself by exploring the rest of the exhibits. Tall shelves were loaded with random items: lunchboxes, dolls, and plaster foot impressions—most meticulously identified via a 1980s-era plastic-punch strip label maker.

In preparation for that private birthday tour, Trav brought home dozens of library books that included local lore as well as heavy academic pieces on the more famous creatures, lovingly suggested by Trav's local librarians.

Adjacent to the Cryptozoology Museum was a secondhand bookstore where Trav purchased a first-edition copy of Sherwood Anderson's *Hello towns!* and he left it on the kitchen table with a note that read, "I love you more than Sasquatch loves apples."

Since I did not understand the reference, Trav patiently explained that Sasquatch sightings happen most often near fruit trees, and the supposition is that Sasquatch must have a sweet tooth.

It was a sincere compliment.

———

Quirky museums like the International Cryptozoology Museum are a shared interest, and as we walked the loop around Cooter's Place, a weirdly curated mix of life-sized cardboard cutouts and television props, I thought about licensing and ownership, wondering who owned the rights to the Dukes of Hazzard brand.

This led to thinking about the ownership of stories in general. Much like the Confederate flag debate, two people can experience the same external symbol with different reactions.

As proof of this, one Boychoir alumnus sent a note, angry at my portrayal of the school. His experience, he insisted, was only positive. His words were sharp, and he insisted that as a writer, I should work to lift up the school, not tear it down.

Again, he did not deny Trav's experience; he just believed his was more important.

Neither experience is truer than the other, but because stories like Trav's are more severe but less common, institutions often present them as less true.

Minimize, deflect, and curate a bigger, shinier, truer truth.

Heritage, not hate.

CHAPTER FOURTEEN
Bluebird & Parnassus

After completing the loop around the strange Dukes of Hazzard Museum display, Trav remembered Parnassus Books was also on our list.

"Let's go get you a book," he said.

Nashville's Parnassus Books is located not in a quaint downtown space I had mythologized from its interior online photos and feature stories in literary magazines. In anticipation of the trip, I had scanned through images of rich, polished, book-filled shelves. The website advertised a long list of author visits and events, and I envisioned a literary oasis.

Instead, the shop is crammed into a corner of Nashville's heavily trafficked Hillsboro Plaza strip mall, and upon arrival I realized how easily myths are built.

"Well," I remarked, still hopeful. "There's easy parking."

The way I understand the Greek mythology, Parnassos was the leader of a city once flooded by torrential rains. During that flood, survivors escaped by climbing a nearby mountain and established a new community on Mount Parnassus, named in honor of the original flooded city's leader. According to tradition, Mount Parnassus became the home of the Muses and the center of Greek poetry, music, and education.

Interestingly, childhood sexual abuse, particularly within the context of a marriage, often feels like running up mountains, dodging floods, and hoping to encounter a Muse. I anticipated a Muse-like connection at Parnassus Books, and this was the impetus for my visit. Ann Patchett, one of the shop's owners, wrote *Truth and Beauty,* about her complicated relationship with author Lucy Grealy.

Lucy was the first instructor I met during my graduate study at Bennington College. That same semester, she overdosed on heroin. When I watched her sway at the lectern on the night of her reading, and I listened to the in-process passages of a clunky rough draft, the literary gods surrounding me suddenly felt human.

This is important because I had spent that first residency intimidated. I sat on Tishman Lecture Hall's hard, stadium-style seats, listened to a presentation on Jorge Luis Borges, and scribbled phonetic approximations of words and phrases I did not recognize: *rubric, frisson, existential ennui.* I bought a pocket dictionary from the campus bookstore that same afternoon.

After that first Borges lecture, I walked back to the dormitory and cried.

I stayed in the room through supper, ate a candy bar from my purse, and waited for the social anxiety to diminish. The next morning, an administrator pulled me into an office and asked some gentle questions, among them a humiliating "Are you making friends?"

———

My Bennington instructors included literary icons, and classmates younger than me had broader publication credits. I still smarted from when Trav had dropped me off at the residence hall, and there was a small party assembled in the common area. A newspaper editor poured wine for a documentarian while a nature writer spoke to a woman living in France. A man from Japan brought us all a tea I could not pronounce.

Trav opened the door and plopped my suitcase down. Then, in a voice level that suggested competing to be heard over road noise and the car stereo on a long drive, he looked both left and right down the hallway and interrupted the quiet academic gathering with a loud "Hey, Shonna, where's the shitter?"

These memories are funny to me now. And those people who once intimidated me? They are now friends who would happily direct Trav to the bathroom facilities.

———

I left northern Maine's potato country at age seventeen after high school graduation. Despite studying English as an undergraduate, I quite literally did not understand this new language of academia.

The graduate program seemed mythical, and I spent those early few days weeping to Trav on the telephone and wanting to leave. I had not yet received a clinical anxiety diagnosis or found a prescription to mitigate the symptoms, so I dulled the panic with leftover painkillers.

I went to bed each night staring at a card Trav had given me when we celebrated my acceptance.

The card showed the back view of a little girl in denim overalls, hoisting herself over a fence railing. "You can do it," Trav wrote.

———

That night at Lucy Grealy's reading, my anxiety began to thaw. While not exactly confident, I arrived early and found a seat on the aisle, figuring that eventually some person would sit next to me. My tendency was to stutter and blurt observations in a manner that can sound angry, insensitive, or mean, and my goal was to avoid doing that.

I also wanted to make a friend.

Lucy's facial deformities, so emotionally detailed in her *Autobiography of a Face*, stood in real-life physical form not twenty feet in front of me. Here, I thought, was an actual person who wrote an important book and who planned to teach me writing skills.

Then I watched her stumble.

Under the lights, her tiny frame seemed frail and imperfect as her voice tripped over the raw sentences. Her skin was pale, her features hollow, and I felt immediate relief that she would guide my first semester of study.

I saw Lucy as more than delightfully human; I also recognized something amiss. Experience with Trav suggested some sort of demon, and while academia felt like a foreign language, I spoke "issues" with fluency. Lucy's feedback that semester was rocky and incoherent, punctuated by bits of lucidity, encouragement, and wisdom. When the program director called to share news of her overdose and death later in that first term, I was not surprised.

———

It was the briefest of connections, but Lucy wore a cowboy hat at our first meeting, and she let me try it on before making a head lice joke. She swore. She projected an enormous and bawdy sense of humor from her sprite-like body.

Later, when I read *Truth and Beauty*, I could formulate a more nuanced vision of my first literary mentor through Ann Patchett's friendship. The woman she described I had met in person, so naturally a trip to Nashville needed to include a visit to this store.

Except the store was smaller than it seemed in the photos, and the space narrower. That perception is a product of my own outsized expectations, though, because the space itself is as warm and homey as its online presence suggests. Naturally, Ann Patchett's books were featured prominently, and I ran my fingers along the spines, happy to be present and trying to decide what to purchase.

Instead of books, I bought a tote bag that would eventually lug a big file of legal paperwork.

"What are our options?" I would later ask our lawyer after receiving the film company's letter, fishing the large stack of papers from the Parnassus Books tote bag and stacking them on the conference room table.

———

Trav wanted that bookstore experience to be monumental for me—a sort of pilgrimage to mimic his own joy at Gruhn Guitars. I did, too. I waited for a spark of inspiration, or connection, or any sensation other than "Hey, I am kind of hungry."

In the absence of this inspiration, I wondered if I was even capable of feeling Trav's level of spiritual connection. I wondered if years of intense work at being a supportive partner to Trav had ground out any inspirational spark in me.

I suspect many partners like me feel the same way.

———

Vic is our psychotherapist. Trav and I call him "Psycho, the Rapist," and although it is a dark, inside joke, breaking the syllables helps with the realization that we are on the lifetime therapy plan. Referring to Vic as "Psycho, the Rapist" makes us both laugh, and in the throes of the grimmest moments, I cling to anything that causes laughter—anything that brings release.

I found Vic through a series of telephone calls and recommendations. I knew he was the right guy when, after I explained the nature of Trav's problems, he took a moment to respond.

"Yes," he said. "It is always much easier when it is only someone else's issue."

I appreciated this dry, witty, and pointed personal observation, and the following week Trav and I were seated on his couch.

Vic is an expert on psychometrics, including the Myers-Briggs Type Indicator. During one session I asked if it was possible for a subconscious battle to occur in relationships between two people with the same four-letter personality traits. I asked, if two similar people mate, will the person with the stronger leanings weaken his or her partner's less pronounced traits and push them further down the scale? Could Trav's extremes diminish my own similar, native character?

Each subsequent personality test showed my fundamental traits inching in opposite directions.

"Yes," Vic said. "That often happens."

―――――

Vic has treated us both for more than a decade now. I have drifted in and out of the counseling room, but Trav has been consistent.

That is another tricky part for partners. When our diagnoses are not as acute, as loud, or as life-threatening, it is easy to step aside and make way for our partners, believing it is the compassionate thing to do.

Often, it is not.

As hard as therapy might be for a male survivor of childhood sexual abuse, Vic maintains it is often even more difficult for a partner. When a partner's role is as the constant and reliable person, on call and ever ready, twenty-four/seven, therapy can seem like a luxury.

"I feel Scotch-taped together," I told Trav when he asked, gently, if it might help for us to make a long-overdue appointment. We were driving to a restaurant at the time, and I remember how the act of socializing away from the house felt like I was letting my guard down in a dangerous way. "I just can't start picking it apart right now."

He reached over to touch my knee in a moment of sincere connectedness, reflective of his fundamental character.

"Then I will help you hold the tape."

―――――

After our Parnassus Books excursion, later that night in Nashville, and recovering from a meal that included even more biscuits, Trav performed onstage at the Bluebird Café. That moment onstage was a natural high that exceeded his blissful afternoon at the guitar store. Although a quick performance, its personal significance was long-lasting and a concrete expression of something mythical.

At the Bluebird, my husband found his Muse.

According to the Bluebird's website, the original owner and founder sold the venue to a not-for-profit organization devoted to the service of songwriters and the craft of songwriting. However, it was the stage itself and not the mission that beckoned Trav. Like Parnassus Books, the performance space was tinier than it seemed in photos, but the energy surrounding it was thick and electric. I thought of other performers who had played that stage, from a chubby and unknown Garth Brooks to Bebe Buell, John Prine, Kix Brooks, the Cowboy Junkies, and Kris Kristofferson.

Trav brought his 1959 Gibson J45. Smooth and brown, this Gibson guitar is a family heirloom purchased by his mom for fifty dollars in 1965 as a present to his father. Not long after Trav told his parents the truth about his experience at the American Boychoir School, Trav's dad gifted him the instrument in a symbolic, powerful gesture. Rich in both color and tone, the guitar impresses enthusiasts, and Trav features it at most of his performances.

When I watched Trav carry his dad's old Gibson onto that historic Bluebird stage and wait for his introduction, I wished his father had been present. I suspect Trav's dad, also a gifted performer, struggles with the Boychoir's effect on his son.

As a parent, how could you not?

———

Even if it was an unpaid, single song in an open-mic setup, Trav wanted to stand on the Bluebird stage with his dad's Gibson in front of an audience. He sweated his song selection on the drive over. He had chosen his shirt, an elaborate, embroidered Western piece. As he ordered coffee and waited his turn, I thought about how he had let whiskey go.

Alcohol negated the therapeutic effect of his particular mix of medications, so Trav cut back and then eliminated it entirely. When Vic mentioned the word *alcoholism,* it surprised Trav to hear the diagnosis.

Trav came home that day depressed.

Because he had never really hit rock bottom, and was never violent or particularly excessive with whiskey, Trav had considered it more of a social lubricant to smooth his performance. He liked the burn in his throat, and he liked the way it softened the edges. The idea that his beloved Wild Turkey and Maker's Mark would become another diagnostic label felt oppressive and overwhelming.

———

The night at the Bluebird was about being heard by an audience that gave a damn, not about pay, but for the joy of the music. This was part of the road trip's goal: to find the joy in music again. And this particular Muse needed to present as part of a sober, unblunted experience.

I was not capable of feeling that level of joy in my mythic bookstore, but I wanted my husband to feel it on his mythic stage.

Once introduced, Trav tripped over his words in a rare display of nerves, but he found his groove quickly, and there was no stopping the crowd reaction once it began. My husband, onstage, becomes an animated, electrified presence. He banters, he reads the room's energy, he teases, and he dances. Most importantly, he delivers a consistent and high-quality product.

But on that night, he was also happy.

He was happy, and the music flowed through his body. In less than four minutes he had checked the event off his list of life goals, and for those four minutes he was making music for the joy.

When Trav took the applause, I stood up and clapped the loudest. Had his dad been there, he would have clapped even louder than me.

Childhood sexual abuse might have dampened his spark, but that night at the Bluebird, Trav felt the electricity return. He felt the electricity, and he channeled that energy through the length of his body.

As he stood on the Bluebird stage, the applause continued to roll toward Trav, and I placed my camera down and began to jump and yell. Sometimes I forget the power of Trav's voice.

He nodded, bowed one last time into the stage lights, and then stepped off the stage. I had asked the server to refill his coffee, and I nearly tipped over the mug with my elbow on the way to hug him tight. His sweaty face pressed into my neck, and I could feel the outline of his smile.

However much his experience at the American Boychoir had dulled his approach to music, Trav's passion was not completely gone.

Later that night in the hotel room after the Gibson had been lovingly polished, Trav strummed quietly in the corner with his new Blue Chip pick from Gruhn Guitars while I read the local newspaper on the hotel bed, surrounded by a nest of pillows.

"Hey," he asked. "Would you listen to something for me?"

Over the years, we have learned that I can be a harsh editor, and Trav must be clear about expectations.

"Sure," I answered, twisting in my pillow nest toward his corner of the room. "What am I listening for?"

"I just want a reaction."

I rested my chin on a pillow, closed my eyes, and waited. Trav strummed a chord progression that would ultimately become the song "Revelation." It was intricate and complex, and I recognized it as the beginning of something powerful after what seemed like a lifetime of running up that Parnassus Mountain hoping to find a Muse.

I opened my eyes when the notes stopped.

"It is beautiful, Trav."

He made eye contact with me, and I nodded.

"Honest."

The energy in our hotel room shifted at that moment, and Trav put the Gibson in its case. Then he pulled back the blankets in his bed and invited me to join him.

CHAPTER FIFTEEN
Alabama February

When I was little, the Funk & Wagnalls Encyclopedia, bought at the grocery store in alphabetical segments for pennies with a food purchase, was my Internet, and it contained a wealth of information within its covers. Some volumes were fatter than others. The S volume, for instance, was much thicker than the Q volume. I loved the encyclopedia smell, and I loved the sensation of pressing the stiff and shiny pages.

Among other fun facts, Funk & Wagnalls taught me that the state of Hawaii is actually a chain of distinct islands, and when I first traveled to the Hawaiian Islands I remembered reading the encyclopedia entry while tucked under a crocheted afghan blanket.

It was the same for Alabama, a state I had never visited before this trip but recalled reading about in the Funk & Wagnalls. I thought about the era before the Internet as we loaded the van and moved from

Nashville toward New Orleans, trying to put my perceptions of the state in order.

———

Trav and I stopped for an overnight stay in Tuscaloosa and, too tired to explore, we brought takeout burritos to the hotel room. In my bed, I studied about Lurleen Wallace while Trav tinkered with the Gibson. While I learned about Mrs. Wallace, Trav strummed chords from old Carter family hymns in the corner. Still high from his Nashville inspiration, Trav was experimenting with songs for his next recording project. He had a vision for the sound, and he played with the arrangements.

———

The wife of Alabama segregationist George Wallace, Lurleen Wallace ran for election as his unofficial proxy when term limits prevented her husband from being reelected. Although she might have been a political figurehead, it was still an office that many traditionally liberal states had failed to bestow upon a woman. To date, she has been Alabama's only female governor, and she governed for just 478 days before dying from a cancer whose diagnosis was, as was customary, withheld from her and relayed only to her husband.

While closely linked to her husband's political agenda, Lurleen Wallace also championed mental health reform. Before she died, she worked to improve Alabama's dismal asylum conditions. Eventually, Alabama would lead the nation in establishing a standard of care for inpatient treatment, but it took a thirty-three-year-long court battle. The tenets of this reform, now known as the "Wyatt Standards" from the case *Wyatt v. Stickney*, include a humane psychological and physical environment, qualified and sufficient staff for administration of treatment, individualized treatment plans, and minimal restriction of patient freedom.

It seems simple and obvious that institutionalized patients should receive a basic, therapeutic standard of care, but perception often gets clearer with hindsight and time. Technology changes, too, and when we know better, we tend to do better.

————

When I was young, that Funk & Wagnalls set from the grocery store showed me the broader world. Now I can carry the entire contents of an encyclopedia with a mobile device that fits into the back pocket of my jeans.

On that Alabama hotel room bed, while I balanced a burrito over the screen where I was researching the asylum process, I thought about progress, and specifically, the progress for people suffering from mental illness and mood disorders and the great leaps in public perception.

Lurleen Wallace assumed this challenge during an era when patients with mental illness were locked up and exposed to inhumane living conditions and when she, as a woman, was kept from her initial personal cancer diagnosis.

As I scrolled through historical details while Trav strummed, I wondered about the future of advocacy for childhood sexual abuse victims, hoping their current treatment will one day be seen as equally as primitive and horrifying as the conditions that led Lurleen Wallace to speak up and push for reform.

————

Right now, Trav's diagnoses rarely describe heroes. His diagnoses: depression, bipolar disorder, alcohol dependence, night terrors, post-traumatic stress disorder, and anxiety. Portrayed as grotesque in films, books, and news stories, these words generally describe the villains.

"Bad guys" on television are often linked to mental illness or mood disorders, and mental health diagnoses often become a default explanation for extreme behavior. It is neither fair nor right, but worse than these sensationalized social depictions of extreme behavior are the small indignities.

Ours is not a life with the highs and lows popularized by the media. Instead, ours are the small mortifications, like when Trav was required to present a note on professional letterhead indicating that his medications would not inhibit operation of a vehicle. Because of his diagnoses, Trav needs a doctor's approval to renew his driver's license. The Department of Motor Vehicles worker was kind in his delivery, but it still stung. On an ordinary day, as Trav completed an ordinary errand while thinking of nothing more extreme than how long he might have to wait in the row of industrial chairs until the number on his paper slip was called, it was one more reminder of the American Boychoir School experience.

———

An estimated one in four women in the United States has experienced childhood sexual abuse. For men, that number is one in six. While these ratios can be compared in a vacuum, victim narratives almost always skew female. Resources for men are few. If the victim is male, the measure of shame and denial involved becomes particularly acute in the absence of this support.

Since sexual trauma nearly always coincides with mental illnesses, if Trav had been born in a different era, his diagnoses might have earned him a spot in a polluted, state-run asylum.

How many men in those early, abysmal state-run asylums, I wondered, experienced childhood sexual abuse? It is impossible to know for certain. What is certain is that it took thirty-three years of litigation for the Wyatt case to manifest into a ruling that established a standard of care.

Thirty-three years.

This must change.

I clicked off my computer and dreamed of Lurleen Wallace that night, wondering what effect, if any, my words might have in the larger conversation about childhood sexual abuse, either in my lifetime or beyond.

———

The next day, on the road once again, I insisted on listening to Emmylou Harris sing "Red Dirt Girl" as we drove past the signs for Meridian, Mississippi, and I reflected on the near-universal experience of small-town origins and the near-universal challenges of mental illness.

"Poor Lillian," I lamented as Emmylou sang about her song character's particular challenges, thinking of all the proverbial Lillians experiencing real-life isolation and depression and wondering how I, like Governor Lurleen Wallace, might use my talent to change that situation.

CHAPTER SIXTEEN
Voodoo

On our first day in New Orleans, when Trav and I were sipping bitter chicory coffee while shivering under the Café Du Monde tent and I was lamenting my current sex life, we were killing time before the voodoo session. In preparation for the trip, we had studied the history and incarnations of the voodoo religion, trading fun facts on our living room couch.

"Marie Leveau had fifteen children with her common-law husband after her first husband disappeared under mysterious circumstances," I warned. "She was also a hairdresser."

Trav countered with "The voodoo portrayal in *Live and Let Die* was pretty much the epitome of sensationalized Western perception. Embarrassing for Bond."

"Say *vodoun*, not voodoo," I challenged. "But with an authoritative accent, like you regularly spell *magic* with a *k*.'"

He did.

I laughed.

Books and the details they contain are a passion Trav and I do share, and he visits the local library each week, choosing titles for me and stacking them on the coffee table. When the librarians look up and see Trav walk through the door, I imagine they feel a little tingle and wonder what topic might be next.

Of recent interest: medical oddities, political biographies, and, in anticipation of this New Orleans travel leg, voodoo history, culture, etiquette, and practice.

What better place, we agreed, to arrange consultation with an expert?

The voodoo shop was a cluttered, colorful space with little altars set up in corner bookshelf nooks. These altars presented, among other scraps infused with symbolism, bits of candy, flower petals, liquor, cigarettes, and jewelry. Transparent glass spice jars lined the wooden shelves, and I inhaled a blend of sweet nutmeg and clove while turning the candles on display to better read their labels: "peace," "money," "passion," "love," and "luck." I found souvenir voodoo dolls, too. Having read about Oshun, the orisha or spirit of fresh water and healing, in advance of the trip, I found her candle as well.

Separated from the store by a low cabinet, the reading space was a simple table and two folding chairs. Our practitioner wore her fingernails long and painted deep indigo blue. "Statement nails," I offered, trying to break the conversational ice. Her curls—bigger than usual, she explained, because of the weather—puffed beneath a gray scarf she tied as a hair band.

I removed the winter cap I had borrowed from Trav, folded it into my lap, and patted my own wet, limp hair apologetically. "Hat head," I said and made myself as small as possible in the space flanked by canisters of dried and fragrant gris-gris supplies, only some of which I recognized—lavender, cinnamon sticks, and sage leaves.

I guessed her age at thirty-five. She called me Michelle and then apologized for misspeaking. I did not disclose that I remembered my mother saying Michelle was a top name choice for me at birth.

She laid out the cards and suggested I was a writer facing some very personal creative blocks, and not to fear—the next book would come. She called me Michelle two more times and apologized after each statement. The reading itself, with those two exceptions—the writer acknowledgment and Michelle connection—felt vague enough to apply to any woman, and I nodded for the entertainment value.

The final sequence puzzled her, though, and she tapped each card, trying to articulate an interpretation. She moved her head to the right and squinted as she pressed the cards with her blue fingernail.

Finally, she spoke.

"You and your husband were matched in this lifetime to accomplish something extraordinary."

We were together for a reason, she said, maintaining an unsettling eye contact.

"Trust that reason."

Since there is no social script for when a voodoo practitioner affirms a troubled marriage, I thanked her, replaced my hat, exited the shop, and then wandered through the French Quarter while Trav had his turn.

Around a nearby corner, I admired an elaborate fetish shop window display and remembered the newlywed couple under the beignet tent. I imagined myself wearing the window mannequin's red patent-leather stiletto boots. Trav might accept stiletto boots as a joke, but he would flinch at the feather boa and cringe at the riding crop or any of the toys on display. He would have no use for the fishnet stockings, and I envisioned the shop's erotic books left dusty and unopened beside those from the library already stacked on our coffee table.

In a city motivated by physical pleasure, I noted my instinct to stuff down desire and back away from the plate-glass window. Nearby was a secondhand bookstore. Those old books were a familiar comfort zone—paperback novels, biographies, and outdated travel guides. I pushed open the door and then puttered through the stacks, running my fingers against the titles while trying to focus on the voodoo practitioner's admonition to trust the purpose of my marriage.

Instead, I thought about those red boots in the shop window.

Many partners of sexual abuse survivors experience similar thoughts. Triggers appear and then disappear. What was sexy a few months ago is now scarily off limits. Forget any candid conversations about fantasy. And when I had brought up the idea of an open marriage, my husband's face shattered.

"No," he said and shook his head. "I do not want that."

For a partner, options are limited.

———

Trav's voodoo reading was more intense, and he did not discuss details until later that night at our little St. Charles apartment rental. His cards emphasized Saint Michael, the patron saint of protectors. That reference appeared frequently, and the practitioner spoke of archangels, strength, and defenders. The voodoo lady told Trav that he had touched true darkness.

It was, he described, "powerful."

Trav requested a Saint Michael medal the next morning.

It was not the request for this medal, but the lead-up that made me cringe. He explained that while meditating, he had experienced a powerful vision. That powerful vision prompted the lyrics for the Nashville chord progression that would later become "Revelation," and he spent the time writing the words in his journal.

As a skeptic and pragmatist, I struggle with metaphysical language and process. We grew up in the same conservative, blue-collar, rural environment where words and actions like "daily meditation" and "powerful vision" are not commonplace.

I struggle, but I try.

"Are you planning to wear this medal like a necklace?" I asked.

Trav's response was a sort of "Duh, yes," and then "Why?"

"Because you are not Catholic, and it is weird."

Trav felt insulted, and I imagined myself explaining a dinner plate-sized medallion to our friends and family. "Oh, that? Trav's new belief system is the result of powerful meditation that followed his thirty-minute consultation with a New Orleans voodoo queen."

I did not see his need, only my own discomfort.

It was the same sensation when Trav commissioned large bear paws to be tattooed on his forearms.

"Those?" I explained straight-faced to friends too shy to ask Trav directly. "They represent my husband's spiritual kinship with the bear."

It gets exhausting, Trav's eccentricities, and some nights I have wished for a husband whose interests do not stretch far beyond a sports team, beer, or the stock market.

I hear friends speak of insatiable partners, and I wonder what that is like—to have my body desired to the point of annoyance. It is, I imagine, how Trav feels in my presence. Like prey.

Even innocuous touch can unnerve him.

"No," I once said, insisting on a hug in our kitchen. "Hugs from your wife are supposed to feel good."

I imagine for Trav, sharing a transformative metaphysical vision with his wife is meant to feel good, too, and not for the first time in our shared life together, I wondered if there might be a partner better suited for my husband.

CHAPTER SEVENTEEN
The Children of Your People

Saint Michael plays a role in Muslim, Jewish, and Christian traditions of being unequivocally on the side of the righteous. "The great prince who stands for the children of your people," reads the book of Daniel. In John Milton's epic poem *Paradise Lost,* Michael led the army against Satan.

Since it was the lead-up to Mardi Gras, we were told by more than one shop owner that law enforcement officers scoop up Saint Michael paraphernalia, given his significance as a protector.

Still, Trav wanted to purchase a Saint Michael medal in New Orleans.

He wanted the medal, and he wanted me to research a retail source. Since these medals were, more often than not, trinkets mass-produced in third-world countries, and we planned to meander for nearly three more weeks through the buckle of America's Bible Belt, littered with Christian swag shops, I suggested it might not be an emergency.

Trav's fixations happen in the manic phases of his trauma-related bipolar disorder. Usually they are mild, like the intense focus on finding a Saint Michael medallion immediately.

For him in the moment, it was a big deal.

"I really want to find a medal while we're in New Orleans."

"No," I answered. "You really want *me* to locate a medal for you."

This pushed the exchange into what Vic calls "perpetual issues." For us, as with many couples in our situation, our perpetual issue is the parent-child dynamic, and I hate it.

During a break from the Saint Michael discussion in the grocery store parking lot, I offered to shop for supplies in anticipation of the next day's departure.

"What do you want?" was answered with an infuriating "Whatever," and I spent ten minutes coaching, mom-style, from the passenger seat.

"Well, would you like water?"

"Yes, I would like some water."

Then me again: "How about some granola bars?"

And him: "Sure!"

Frustrated, I retreated into a silence that extended to bedtime. I wanted to call a friend or family member, but there were few in my community who knew the extent of our situation, so I sat on the rental apartment couch alone, crunching Zapp's potato chips.

———

Typing these sentences feels disloyal.

All Trav's eccentricities help him navigate his reality, and I support any step toward healing. I support them, and they frustrate me. I reminded myself that many, many things can be true simultaneously.

It is also tricky to write about our life, because when Trav is in the right headspace I feel like the luckiest woman in the world. Every day, we laugh. Not just smiles, but loud and big-bellied laughs. Even in the midst of arguments, we can push a pause button to observe some random hilarious moment.

That is what makes childhood sexual abuse so difficult to address: no hard-and-fast rules. There is no chemotherapy consultation for which the risks are weighed by experts, and then a treatment plan is established. There is no surgical solution or miracle pill to swallow.

Trav was still smarting about my reluctance to prioritize a Saint Michael medal at breakfast the next day, but we brokered a fragile peace and found Elizabeth's Restaurant, a Bywater neighborhood joint not far from Desire and Piety Streets. Because I love wordplay, I noted our location near Congress Street and not far from Independence Street.

The sun started to break the unusual February cold snap. We had just received biscuits and eggs with Elizabeth's famous candied praline bacon, and since the mood seemed lighter after a night of sleep, we discussed the wall art.

The bright acrylic paint on wood by a local artist called Dr. Bob blended folk art and found items with an outsider flair. The smaller pieces in particular captivated both of us. They were simple and cheap wood frames, available for purchase at any craft store, but Dr. Bob had painted them in electric pink and green colors, stapled unique bottle caps along the edges, and written life advice in the center in bold black marker.

"No selling cats" and "Be nice or get bitten" were my favorites.

As the sun made the metal flatware sparkle, any remaining tension between us seemed to break, and we loved Dr. Bob's wisdom: "Be nice or leave."

———

Approximately $300 in Trav's shirt pocket were singles left over from his last gig before we had left Maine, and these made a substantial bundle. When the check arrived, he removed this money to pay for breakfast, and in doing so gestured toward Dr. Bob's wall of art in a sweeping motion, using the fanned cash as a makeshift pointer.

There was nothing discreet about his money waving, and the gesture struck me as obnoxious. Not so much dangerous, as the crowd at Elizabeth's seemed more hipster-hungover than thief, but it felt conspicuous, and I whispered to tuck away the wad.

That is when Vic's assessment of the perpetual issue hits again. As much as I hated being the parent, Trav hated being the child even more. There was a sharp intake of breath, and a very emphatic hiss of "No."

Trav's face was now red.

"Do not treat me like I am a child."

His reaction seemed disproportionate to the situation, and that is our constant dynamic: assessing what is illness and what is legitimate concern.

Plus, it pissed me off.

"Even when you act like a child?" was my initial reaction, but years of therapy had taught me to rephrase. That noted, even the rephrase sounded bitchy. "What is your preferred response when you behave in a way that is obnoxious?"

"If it is not hurting anyone else," Trav spoke earnestly, his voice now lowered. "I'd like you to let it go."

Letting go of things has never been my specialty. I fired back about my responsibility to purchase groceries and to arrange hotel rooms with multiple locks, a chair to brace the doorknob, window shades to darken the space, and two separate beds. And, most recently, to research his new embrace of voodoo Catholicism while reminding a grown man not to wave a fan of cash over his head.

Sometimes the healing process is scary, and sometimes it is absurd.

Sometimes, it is rage making.

I excused myself to the restroom, upstairs through a bar area decorated with more of Dr. Bob's art, this time a large, elaborate alligator scene. When I sat, fully clothed, on the toilet, I thought of how Trav had accidentally cracked the rental apartment's toilet seat, and since the contract was in my name, it would be my responsibility to address.

I rested my forehead on my hands, stared at the floor, and tried to sort out the source of my anger, wondering how this particular discord might affect my husband's mental health.

———

The sink's lukewarm water ran over my hands, and after crumpling the paper towel, I slammed it into the wastebasket. Then I smacked the wall with my palm.

I had, literally, hit a wall.

We paid the bill without purchasing a Dr. Bob original, and then poked through the Piety Street market without speaking on the way back to the car. None of the crafts, soaps, or musty-smelling vintage clothing inspired us, and I tried to sort the trauma-related from the typical marriage annoyance.

That is the trickiest part: figuring out cause and effect. It is also a matter of placing value. Am I reacting to my husband being an ass? Or am I unfairly putting expectations on a man who is struggling to maintain an uneasy equilibrium?

Or am I the ass here? It is, quite often, hard to delineate.

We approached the van, and he held the door open while I boosted myself inside. Trav and I were matched in this lifetime to accomplish something extraordinary, the voodoo lady had told me, and at that moment I could not imagine a bigger pile of bullshit.

CHAPTER EIGHTEEN
Florida Riviera

Compassion, not blame.

These concepts are simpler in retrospect than they are in the moment, and we spent the six hours between New Orleans and Panama City Beach pissed off and staring at the road, neither of us saying a word.

I tried to make light with camera selfies, and when Trav showed no response beyond his tightened jaw, I moved back to indignant silence.

At that moment, I also calculated the cost of a flight home. A quick spreadsheet could split the debt and assets equally. If I called ahead, divorce papers could be waiting with the house on the market by the time Trav returned in the van. The cats for Trav, the dog for me. Trav could have the new computer, too.

With details fair and equitably organized, my mind was free to design the next steps. I would likely relocate, but where? A brick, urban walk-up seemed as appealing as an off-season beach rental. Northern California topped the list. Hawaii and Boston, too. A radical change might be better, though, and I wondered about the difficulty of easing into the Swedish language and culture. Friends in Australia would welcome me.

Ultimately, the golden hills and vineyards along the drive to Calistoga won, and I settled on the San Francisco region. I could double my income, and all debt could be gone within a year if I was willing to live simply. Of course, I would still communicate with Trav. In my mind, we would be friendly exes.

I imagined him dating a fleshy, smiling woman from a local mill town. She would likely have a child or two already, knowing that Trav would make an excellent stepfather. Trav's new girlfriend would come out to Trav's shows and be thrilled if he showed up at her house on time with a pizza, bottle of diet soda, and ice cream for the kids.

Yes, I believed at that moment, Trav would be much better suited to a woman like that. A simple woman with simple expectations and simple needs.

The trouble with an active imagination and six long, stony-silent hours is that by the time we found our Panama City Beach hotel, I had logged every detail of our breakup and subsequent relationships. The girlfriend of my ex-husband, I decided, would hang a high school graduation tassel from her turquoise hatchback. The car would smell like a Yankee Candle vanilla air freshener, and Trav would be too polite to tell her vanilla scents nauseate him.

While Trav was developing this new relationship, I would run down my list of exes and angle for fantastic break-up sex, cull my belongings, and then drive across the country with my nervous, wire-haired terrier mix. When I hit the Pacific Ocean, I would stop.

It was done, and I had decided. I researched the closest airports, and I would tell Trav about the plan that night.

———

We were fighting about toilets now, and our voices escalated. Our voices rarely got this loud, but I was pissed off because he clogs up toilets. I deflected to the physics argument again, noting that the diameter of the toilet pipe is a good indicator of the quantity it can absorb. This is because, in addition to cracking the seat, Trav had clogged the toilet at the New Orleans rental, too.

He had just clogged the toilet again in our Panama City hotel, and when I heard the tell-tale gurgle of water, I was ready to forgo the return flight and just walk home from Florida's panhandle to Maine.

I was done. Done, done, done.

I wanted nothing more at that moment than to tie my shoes and go. Having not smoked in decades, I wanted a cigarette, a bottle of gin, and to get laid. I wanted a husband who possessed the foresight to flush the damned toilet when it was reasonably full and before it overflowed, and who could sit still on a toilet seat without cracking it.

I wanted to step outside my life and get myself back on track in an existence that did not involve a level of supervision that rivaled that of a toddler or infant. I wanted to cease tracking Trav's sleep patterns, open the window at night, and wake to sunlight from a bedroom window.

Trav finally spoke. "Do you think I enjoy breaking toilet seats?"

I didn't know what to say to this because part of me thinks he does enjoy the entertainment factor. It is part of his bon vivant persona, and if a toilet seat gets cracked, then c'est la vie! It is another example of how Trav's big personality can suffocate because somebody—me—must be present to either explain the obvious to him or apologize on his behalf.

In that moment I was balancing on the edge of the hotel bed physically, and again metaphorically, as I watched Trav sit in the ugly, patterned corner armchair.

He was angry, too, and part of me liked it. It was some emotion, and it was better than the past six hours of silence.

This was the point in the fight when Trav lobbed my own criticisms back at me, and in the moment he was not quite hollering, but his voice had an elevated pitch, and he was gesturing for emphasis.

I could not hear him through my own rage. Because of the silent six hours, I had already researched Maine's divorce process, and I just needed to get back to set it all in motion. Forty-eight hours, I estimated. That was all I needed to get away from this.

I imagine many other partners like me experience similar bouts of rage. At that moment in the Panama City Beach hotel room, I did not care about Trav's list of needs. I cared about mine, and at the top of my list was getting the hell away from the existence I felt in no way equipped to handle.

"I have used a LOT of public toilets and NOT overflowed them!"

Trav's words jolted my thought process because he said them with the same authority, expertise, and conviction of a politician.

He held his hand up for emphasis, and then slammed it down on the chair's arm with the fervor of an evangelical preacher.

I would later see the same gesture when he slammed his hand down during the visit to the lawyer's conference room table, the same meeting where I pulled neatly indexed files from my Parnassus Books tote bag.

"Nobody," Trav said, "calls my wife a liar."

This meeting was in response to the film company's legal representative sending me a cease-and-desist letter. After the onslaught of positive media attention for the film, I wrote an essay about the unsavory and scary implications this film promised for my family.

Then I wrote a letter to the film's producers asking for a conversation. This, I thought, might raise the dialogue about child sexual abuse, story ownership, and artistic license and creative responsibility. The impact, I thought, could be tremendous.

When one of the producers agreed to a telephone conversation, I had the same nervous sensation as when I had spoken to the American Boychoir School's acting president.

But I never expected to be blown off.

When this producer did not call as planned, I sent a follow-up note, asking if I misunderstood the time. The producer apologized and rescheduled. That conversation got blown off, too.

So much information is available online. It was easy to collect contact information for other people affiliated with the film, such as film festival directors, actors, theater companies, and relevant industry publications.

I sent a version of the original letter to a dozen or so of these affiliates.

I received a note from a Canadian cinema company addressing my concerns but explaining that for them it was an issue of censorship, and they preferred to let audiences decide the merits of the film itself. I respected that position and appreciated the communication.

The Cannes Film Festival representative was brief in response. "The film will not be part of the next Cannes Film Festival."

The cease-and-desist letter arrived just before Christmas.

"Cease and desist" sounds hostile in print, and the letter outlined the film company's potential for financial harm because of my words. To connect a fictional boy choir film with a real school that provided actors, music, and promotion was, the lawyer noted, "irrational."

"Be careful," friends advised. "These people will protect their investment."

When the letter arrived, my belly churned, but my first thought was to note its poor construction and grammar. Had this lawyer been one of my students, I would have circled the errors, marked it with a C, and offered to reconsider a revision.

But this was not a student.

"My client has no statement regarding the allegations involving the American Boychoir School as they are not affiliated or involved in the school in any way," read the letter.

———

Trav's angry scene in the lawyer's office did not quite match his elevated pitch in the Panama City Beach hotel room, but it was close.

So was the absurdity.

How do two people who once worked in the potato fields of northern Maine's Aroostook County end up paying a lawyer to outline options when a Hollywood film company sends a legal directive to cease and desist?

It was the kind of random life experience I sought, but turned upside down in Bizarro fashion.

"Be careful what you wish for" is the ancient adage, and it is true. I had wished for an artistic man with an accent, never imaging that would manifest as a country musician with a northern Maine accent. I had dreamed my writing might reach a large audience, never expecting that audience to be a group of childhood sexual abuse victims and their families.

The absurdity reached its peak in that Panama City hotel room when, continuing his impression of an evangelical preacher, Trav gesticulated to an extreme.

"I have used a LOT of public toilets!" he repeated. "And a LOT of toilets in general."

I could tell it struck Trav as absurd, too. His hand, once in midair, dropped to his lap, and during the pause I started to smile.

The smile turned into a laugh, and the laugh broke the tension.

Trav laughed, too. Since it is impossible to remain serious in the presence of his hysterics, I laughed even harder.

"Have you, now?"

We both re-created the gesture and the passionate emphasis.

Recalling the Loveless Café conversation, I asked if he had eaten more pigs or used more toilets.

He said that was a stupid question.

By the time we caught a breath, it was too late to find food, as most of the Panama City Beach area was closed for the night. Although the hotel smelled musty and depressing with its low ceilings and ugly wall art, it felt safe, so we unpacked our granola bars and each took a bed.

In the morning, with hindsight and rest, the long, stony drive and resulting fight seemed far away and inconsequential. Trav showered, and then it was my turn. I brushed my teeth while wrapped in a towel, trying to remember what the fuss was all about and why it seemed worth such an extreme level of discord.

Of course, I did not want to divorce this man.

"Did you hear that?" Trav's voice called from behind the bathroom door while I laid out clothing from my bag, and I congratulated him on his double flush. Rather than annoying, the gesture seemed charming, because in his way, with that extra toilet flush, Trav was moving toward me.

CHAPTER NINETEEN
Panama Beachcombers

S quinting in the Florida daylight, we drove down Panama City Beach's main drag to orient ourselves and agreed that the current hotel, while adequate, was ill situated. It was another metaphor. Neither of us wanted to settle for "adequate"—on this trip and also in life. We wanted the full, concentrated, gritty, gaudy Panama City Beach hum.

We debated options at a Waffle House table set with finely grated hash browns and harsh, bracing coffee. Waffle House is a southern phenomenon, not unlike a Duane Reade on every New York City corner or the popularity of Dunkin' Donuts in Boston. The décor is a consistent palette of yellow, black, and deep orange, and we aspired to be as funky and lacking in self-consciousness as the many elderly couples who shared the dining area and flipped through the heavy laminated menus.

The Florida panhandle in February, we realized, had a variety of last-minute lodgings. Full of food and looking down the long strip of waterfront options, we diverted the van into the Beachcomber, a behemoth pink high-rise. While the hotel was not luxurious, its location on the beach meant it was undeniably well placed. Trav and I talked about smart growth and building permits, seasonal population density increases, and the general condition of the environment in the state.

If I had to pick the moment where the mood—and, in a sense, our entire marital outlook—shifted, it was when we relocated to the Beachcomber. Part of being an adult is knowing when to take a loss and when to deviate from the plan. By forfeiting the first hotel's remaining lodging cost, we gained a stocked kitchenette, sitting room, and balcony that overlooked the long stretch of vacant powdery-sand beach.

I remained in the van while Trav negotiated a rate. Proud, he returned waving a key card. When the first room did not suit him, it was Trav who handled a switch with the desk clerk. It was Trav who sorted out the financial and logistical details while I leaned back in the passenger seat and unfolded a newspaper.

Trav had been the one to sort out his security needs, and any annoyance or blowback did not affect me. Excited—truly excited—for the first time in the journey, I opened the balcony doors. My only job was to open those balcony doors, feel the ocean air, and watch the horizon. Although frigid by Florida standards, the breeze brought memories of late Maine springs. As the afternoon sun melted into every shade of pink and orange, I wrapped a loose shirt over a camisole and set a plate of munchies on the little table.

Trav and I have eaten some excellent meals together, including one curated, seven-course dining experience that lasted for nearly four hours with butter-poached lobster and cave-aged prosciutto. We have shared artisanal approaches to pizza, bought expensive cheese, and dipped into the molecular gastronomic aspects of food, too.

Eating well is a priority and an activity we share. Every Sunday night in our home is a celebration of what Trav calls "Free Eat Day," not for the cost but for the guiltless approach we take. Our regular weekday meals include at least three veggies with a seafood or plant-based protein. This menu might include a frozen fruit juice pop, but sweets generally happen in the form of fresh fruit or yogurt. No extra salt. No hydrogenated fats. Limited white flour and white sugar.

Trav's health improves with a regulated diet.

Sunday, however, is the day for indulgence. Fried clams dockside or drunken Thai noodles on the couch; it does not matter. For as long as we have been a couple, Sunday has been the day for reconnection. If sex happens, it is usually a Sunday. We take the dog for a beach walk, we drive to the lighthouse, we hunt for sea glass like funny old people, or we stay home. Neither of us book work on Sundays.

At the time of our trip we had nearly fourteen years of these Sundays, fourteen years of "Free Eat" days where I could sit opposite Trav at a table and talk.

At the Beachcomber, our balcony chairs were plastic, and we used fingers to peel slices of cheap provolone, but sitting with Trav in that orange Florida light felt like we were the richest people in the world enjoying a decadent feast instead of a box of cheap crackers and a bag of deli cheese.

At that moment, a pod of dolphins swam by with their pups, each one making an arc into the water and out again.

"Did you see that?" I stood up and pointed.

It was another random and surreal moment. Twenty-four hours after sketching out our divorce terms, I watched baby dolphins darting in the ocean.

Trav reached for my hand and pulled me back to the chair beside him. We sat in those chairs until the sky went dark, holding hands and sharing the kind of silence that was the exact opposite from the angry silence of the day before.

We shared a nighttime swim in the hotel pool, too, and then another long stretch of conversation in the hot tub, watching the stars. My stiff neck had disappeared, and all I saw was the shadow of the most interesting man I have ever known, sinking deep in the bubbles.

———

"You are one of those creatures whose coat gets shinier and fluffier in sunny weather," Trav observed the next morning after making the effort to rise a little earlier than usual. He found me on the balcony, reading in the sunshine.

I watched more dolphins swim past for most of the morning, and I looked up at Trav, who leaned against the railing, standing against the morning light. The dolphins excited him, too, and his features seemed softer as well. Not weaker or squishier, but energetically more appealing. I noticed that he, too, is one of those creatures whose coat gets shinier and fluffier in the sunshine.

CHAPTER TWENTY
Congregation of Alligators

When it was time to move out of our little oceanfront condo, I felt emotional and did not want to leave the happy bubble we had created. We smiled more. Trav admired the dress I chose. He touched my waist during a walk through a state park where we watched a single alligator sun himself on distant rocks. For the past twenty-four hours there had been no talk of sex abuse or its effects, and I wanted to keep us in that space.

We loaded the van, and I tried to stay present. That, for me, is always the toughest task. Since what goes up inevitably goes down, it seems counterintuitive not to anticipate the next fall.

The drive east across Florida was a study in introspection. From the passenger window I watched a cluster of convicts, minus any chains, doing trash cleanup along the side of the road in their striped Liberty Correctional Institution pants. We drove past a row of trailer homes by the railroad tracks just outside Juniper, and but for the different type of pine tree, the country landscape could have been rural Maine. A red shirt on a clothesline near those trailers fluttered like a little beacon of hope and familiarity, and I turned my head in the van to watch it for as long as possible.

Bigger thoughts bubbled, and I wondered about the faded Pedro Mart and the Mexican goods store just before the junction of the road with Highway 10. It was rural and isolated, and I imagined the people who lived there. If a person's native landscape consisted of convicts, a clothesline, a trailer park, and a Pedro Mart, would it be easy to hop on that road out of town? Would it be satisfying to remain?

———

Fans of personal responsibility, Trav and I both consider our lives the product of choices as much as environment. Both of us made plans, considered our priorities, and moved in that direction.

As with switching hotels, experience is entirely dependent upon your ability to recognize what can be changed. Staying mired in a shitty hotel room, a shitty headspace, or an isolated little town needed to be a choice.

Childhood sexual abuse steals choices, and that is among the most difficult aspects of it.

———

When we arrived at Amelia Island and then navigated the greater vicinity, we saw signs for the St. Augustine Alligator Farm Zoological Park.

"Want to see 2,700 alligators?" Trav asked.

Of course, I said yes.

The park advertises 2,700 alligators, and that is what Trav's diagnoses and process feel like sometimes: No choice but to navigate a swamp full of alligators. Interestingly, a group of alligators is called a congregation.

By the time we had wandered the length of the sanctuary, around various pools and over footpaths, we had seen a congregation that rivaled any Sunday-morning service, even in the most cavernous of megachurches. The sharp-toothed reptiles, known for eating dogs in the wild, sunned their pointy and ridged backs in a languid display. Every few moments, one would slip into the water to join another that we had not yet noticed.

Just a sheet of hard, waist-high plastic fencing separated us from those creatures piled tightly next to each other, their skin touching and eyes open.

Most unnerving were the albino alligators sent from the Louisiana bayous with their cloudy, milk-toned faces and eerie, rose-colored eyes. I stared at the creatures and thought about how, like diagnoses associated with childhood sexual abuse, albino traits in humans almost always describe the villains in stories. From Daphne du Maurier's *Jamaica Inn* to Dan Brown's *The Da Vinci Code,* there are few positive social depictions.

Unlike albino humans, however, rare albino alligators are said to bring good fortune to those who look directly into their eyes. Desiring all the luck I could get, I tried to make eye contact while the albino alligators kept their positions slow and steady behind the viewing wall.

I thought about how strange it was for us to be there at all. Neither of us has much interest in reptiles.

———

The decision to take this trip was made in June the year prior. Summer ended and winter crept up with no itinerary. Trav and I fell into established roles, which meant that if we wanted to go, it would be me making the plans.

Trav says this is because I am better at it, and he's right. I am. I also enjoy the planning process, but there's a bit of bitterness, too. Well before that moment in the New Orleans grocery store parking lot or the angry drive to Panama City Beach, the perpetual issue had manifested in the form of me snapping the computer closed in disgust because of Trav's contentment to have me do the research.

"I've been doing this work for years," Vic once said, "and you two are probably in the top 5 percent of married couples I see."

When I asked for clarification, he noted our connection, mutual respect, compatibility, effort to communicate, desire for each other's happiness, and genuine affection.

I made a joke about being marriage valedictorians, and that somehow made me feel less of a cliché. I suspect many couples feel like therapy clichés. The couch, the copay, and the sitting with hands gently folded in the lap—there is a prescribed sensation to the experience.

The truth is, a truth I must acknowledge, that in addition to that genuine affection and respect, Trav and I share a dog-on-bone fixation on making our marriage work. Neither of us is willing to let issues erode the relationship.

It was in this spirit that I started pulling at Trav's reluctance to plan and organize. In an attempt to reframe his perspective, I saw less reluctance and more trust. Fundamentally, Trav trusts me to know what we both enjoy. He trusts me to find the best bargains, and he trusts me to keep his issues in mind when making arrangements.

In exchange, he does nearly all the physical driving so I can stare at the horizons, share random trivia, rest my head against the window, and sleep. I trust him to keep me safe on the long highway.

I make the plans, and he implements them.

It is an equal exchange, when I reframe it.

It is also a privilege to help sort his everyday life details. As with planning, I excel at minutiae and keeping perspective. Medications that might work suddenly do not, and nothing heals on the first try. I am good at keeping track, seeing patterns, and drawing the connections.

Every day, Trav must move his body. Every day, Trav must give up to a larger power and center his mind with meditation. Food matters. It is a simple principle, but if junk goes in, his body reacts. No liquor. Yoga nidra has been positive for him, as have shamanic approaches. Chiropractic is more effective than acupuncture. Next on the list to try is float therapy.

He also manages symptoms with pharmaceuticals. Since 2001, Trav has experimented with a long list of different medications and combinations of these medications. For us, this is the trickiest and most frustrating process, and it can feel exactly like approaching a swamp of 2,700 alligators.

———

When Trav wakes in the middle of the night, he never hurts me physically, except for the time he choked me. It sounds pretty bad when I type it.

Trav was having success sleeping with a common prescription medication, and after a few weeks of excellent sleep, he felt optimistic. The medication had its side effects, most notably a moment when Trav bumped his head on the nightstand and, rubbing the scratch, said he believed there were splinters on his forehead that needed extraction. He fixated on these imaginary splinters and then felt the need to urinate.

We bumbled to the toilet, both of us unsteady—him from the disorientation and me from trying to maneuver my large and wobbly husband down the stairs from our bedroom to the bathroom.

It was a funny story in the morning, as Trav had zero recollection of it. He was, he noted, just grateful for the restful sleep. It was a good moment for us, lightly retold in the same way a person might laugh at a night of overindulgent alcohol excess.

Given the excellent rest, even with occasional loopy moments, this particular medication gave us both hope.

That hope lasted until one morning when I reached across his snoring form to adjust our shared alarm clock. The motion prompted a primal response, and within an instant, Trav was alert and pushing my throat against our headboard with his hand wrapped tightly around my neck.

"Hey, hey," I whispered, struggling to inhale. "It's me."

The moment, me immobile and unable to breathe because Trav intended to choke me out, took a second for my brain to process. The full force of his strong arm pinned my throat, and I tapped his shoulder.

"You're okay," I whispered again, feeling his fingers squeeze my neck.

Upon hearing my voice, Trav paused, relaxed his grip, and fell back into the pillow. Within ten seconds, he was snoring again.

Shaken, I left our bed and poured a glass of water in the kitchen while rubbing the sore red spot on my neck where Trav's gentle hand had tried to strangle me ten minutes prior. The sun was just beginning to rise, and I crawled onto the couch but did not sleep, choosing to stay alert and watch the sky lighten through the window.

I weighed options.

I could tell Trav about the encounter, knowing that this medication was very effective for sleep. Or, I could not mention it and hope that my husband would never accidentally kill me in our bed. I could sleep in the guest room, far away if the night terrors came, or I could risk my own physical safety.

Later, when Trav walked down the stairs, stretching and happy, I was working in our office, and he kissed my head good morning. Gone were the telltale bluish circles under his eyes. This medicine worked. It gave him rest, and I resented my impossible decision.

When I told him, Trav's face registered a level of horror.

He asked if I was kidding, as if it were a weird sort of joke I might think funny. I assured him not. "Why would I lie?"

He looked at his hands, asked me to review the series of events, and nodded as I detailed the key points. To reset the alarm clock, I reached over his body, and on instinct he choked my neck against the headboard.

He found the pill bottle, pulled off its cap, and flushed the contents.

———

Treatment is a high-stakes crapshoot, and the process is maddening. For us, there is a ritualistic process of things that work—and a commitment to those things. When each new sex abuse scandal makes headlines,

I feel for the victims, but I scan the story for their partners, wanting to know what's in their medicine cabinets. What antipsychotics had the best results? Did the adrenaline blockers work? Anxiety or depression? Both?

I researched blueberry diets, EMDR, Himalayan salt lamps, and shamanic healing. I read a study about the video game Tetris and its positive effects on certain post-traumatic stress disorder patients. There are treatments involving LSD, MDMA, ketamine, and yoga nidra. I've collected studies on nearly every new mental health drug and its side effects. Ask me about pharmaceutical interactions, and I will list fun facts like how grapefruit changes the way enzymes are broken down in the body, and how this can make blood levels of certain medications dangerously high—even lethal.

When people ask what it is like, I usually shrug and say some version of "not so bad." If pressed, I'll add a convincing "really."

What I do not say is that in addition to the easy list of never again sharing grapefruit with brown sugar or sipping a cool vodka sea breeze, I once spent the evening researching inpatient facilities. While I do not believe Trav would benefit from a closed, insular, and institutional environment, I wanted to bring all options up for consideration.

"If you couldn't stay with me, I am not sure how well I'd do." Trav said this as a way to show my importance, but all I feel is the weight. And then, as if he can read the thoughts in my brain, he says, "I will not be a burden to you."

I don't like those implications, so I repeat the same thing I say to people when they ask, a flip reassurance. "Oh, you're not so bad."

And he's not.

More importantly, he is worth it.

He says he feels like a giant man baby, and again, I say no to reassure him, but both of us can see the similarities. I buy his clothing, I fix his meals, and I get less uninterrupted sleep than the mom of a newborn.

"Bipolar" is the scariest diagnosis, largely because of the images the phrase conjures: cocaine binges, prostitutes, spending sprees. For us, it is less extreme. Quirky, not scary. There is a period of acute fixation, and then a phase of depression. During Trav's fixations, he can be extraordinarily productive. Our rugs get vacuumed, his bookkeeping is current, and he will blow through a stack of library books. During the refractory period, he is sadder and more introspective. He's more likely to watch television and feel blue.

It really is not that bad.

Still, there's a stigma and a shame to the phrase. Add two levels to the clinical assessment, bipolar I and II, and it becomes even worse. We are grateful for manageable highs and lows with shorter extremes between them.

No professional can isolate the causes of all bipolar disorders for certain, but most agree on genetic or hereditary predisposition. Environmental stimuli, however, have a direct causal relationship. Childhood trauma, particularly sexual trauma, tops that environmental stimuli list.

In Trav's case, he likely started with a genetic predisposition for depression. From there, he experienced a variety of childhood sexual abuse-related situational factors. As is common, that experience manifested in post-traumatic stress disorder, which led to treatment for depression and anxiety.

That is when the bipolar disorder diagnosis came.

But I still find myself reassuring people that it is the *good* kind, until I check my prejudices, and I check my privilege. I suspect many partners do the same. "Well, my man might have issues, but at least they are not *those* issues."

It is the same as "molestation lite." Any mental illnesses carry a stigma that elicits the same response.

There is no "good kind."

Still, "I am cycling kind of hard" are not words you want to hear when your husband with bipolar disorder is about two weeks off one of his lighter medications in an attempt to reduce the chemical input.

It makes me sad to watch him fixate in a manic cycle. The manic part of his bipolar disorder looks like electrical outlets. Two outlets were dead in our bedroom, which prompted eight hours of perseveration until Trav fixed them. Same for when the water heater broke. Same for the winter ice dams on our roofline.

Trav's mania manifests in an "I need to do this right now" compulsion that had him, instead of calling around to see if roof rakes are in stock, needing to visit every hardware store and check in person. Instead of ten minutes on the phone, three hours of driving felt right. When the drive time threw off his schedule and made him run late, his anxiety increased.

To help, I will send him a quick to-do list that might look like this:

- Locate passport renewal application forms.
- Buy a printer ink cartridge.

He appreciates these lists, but I must remember to place the items in the correct order. Instead of "I am already near the mall, and the office supply store is right here, so I'll get those ink cartridges," he will drive home to regroup and find the passport renewal forms if that tops the list.

———

I have learned to adjust expectations. I rarely set hard-and-fast departure times, and I rarely wait for Trav's arrival. For instance, I recently asked what time he wanted supper, and he said 6:00 P.M. At 6:30, he called to say he would be home by 7:00. At 7:00, he said 7:30.

I sent a response that supper would be on the stove, and I was heading to the gym. I was disappointed to miss dinner with him, but said I loved him, and if he left for work before I returned, I hoped his show went well.

When I returned from the gym, Trav was standing in the kitchen, and his apology seemed disproportionately self-flagellating. He was nearly in tears.

"You made this beautiful dinner for us to share, and I've disappointed you again." He sighed. "I wasn't where I said I would be."

We talked about perspective and how it sometimes feels like he's Alice hiking through Wonderland. We talked about medication. And what he needed to get through the night. And how it was a good idea to push up his appointment with Vic.

When Trav experiences this headspace, he describes it as beyond quirky or unhappy, as if his being is profoundly off-kilter and his "doing well" is still pretty fucked up.

So when a well-intended person begins with "Have you thought about [any particular solution]," my answer is typically yes. Yes, yes, and fucking yes.

Often nothing works. That is the hardest part, when nothing works.

I gave up trying to find solutions that work, much like when Trav asked me to please not ask him how he slept each morning and to please accept that he would likely never sleep well. So I shifted my perspective.

Vic calls it radical acceptance, and it has helped.

Now, instead of focusing on what heals in capital letters, I try finding things to ease the situation. Even if it is just a tiny, minuscule bit easier, progress in centimeters still reflects progress. "I hope the night moves quickly" is the advice a friend gave me when I shared my fears, and I often return to that statement. Instead of the more common "one day at a time" approach, I prefer "one night at a time." Nights that move quickly are the best.

———

I often wake in the space that is beyond night, but not quite morning enough. If Trav is sleeping beside me, I recapture these hours, lulled by the sound of his light snoring and comforted by his dim shape.

When he is absent, my brain kicks into assessment mode, and I listen for any soft sounds in the office beneath our bedroom. Sometimes I can hear the click of computer keys or his body shifting in the red velvet chair as he watches some silly situation comedy. I imagine him pulling the patchwork quilt stitched by my mother over his legs, and I can settle back into my pillow. Soon, I know he will fold the quilt over the chair, taking care to move as softly as possible up the stairs.

I do not worry that he will wake me anymore. It is the quiet I fear.

———

Progress in centimeters is still progress. I thought about this while walking the winding paths for the length of 2,700 alligators at the St. Augustine Alligator Park and lingering in front of the albinos. Using people-first language by putting the person before the disability, I revised it to "alligators with albinism" and thought about the progress of mental illness stigma. While people with albinism are still represented in an overwhelmingly negative way, a quick Internet search yields a long, long list of celebrities who purportedly are diagnosed with bipolar disorder and other mental illnesses.

Childhood sexual abuse now, too.

Progress in centimeters is progress.

CHAPTER TWENTY-ONE
Lost in the Book Mine

With the store's advertised two million-book inventory—98 percent used and 2 percent new—I was sure I could add a copy of the 1970s' *Liberace Cooks! Recipes from His Seven Dining Rooms* to my collection of strange cookbooks from somewhere in the 55,000 square feet of Jacksonville's Chamblin Bookmine retail space. This random detour, suggested by a high school classmate, turned out to be one of the best aspects of the trip.

In 1976, according to the store's website, Ron Chamblin apparently bought fifteen boxes of books and opened his Bookmine in a tiny Herschel Street shop, expanding the inventory each year and changing locations when the stock outgrew the space. Now with two retail locations and warehouses to hold the overflow, Chamblin Bookmine is consistently ranked among the best bookstores in the United States. In this epic and winding maze of books, if I could not find the Liberace cookbook, I was hoping to at least distract myself from the highway driving.

My interest in Liberace originated from two great aunts. Long dead now and never married, they were postwar sisters who shared a tidy little house. I visited them as a child, and during those long afternoons the two sisters would cluck about my cuteness, pass me quarters, and watch as I sat at their kitchen table trying to not eat the old-lady food prepared for me. "I'm just not very hungry," I explained, pushing soft cucumbers around the plate of warm vinegar with a tiny, antique fork.

After my hands were washed and fingernails inspected, the Liberace admiration began. A pristine souvenir program book from a performance they had once attended was handled with reverence, and we lingered on each smooth and shiny page, tracing the outfits and noting details. Liberace's costumes were peacock blue, yellow, and white. Trimmed with feathers and crystals, Liberace waved from the stage, a brilliant-colored ring wrapping each finger.

"Ermine," my great aunt said as she nodded toward the photo of Liberace's fur-trimmed cape. "It is real ermine."

They replayed his entire show to me from their memories, each one noting different aspects of it.

"He asked us if we liked his outfits," one of them remembered.

"He was so considerate," the other agreed.

As a child, I loved every page of the game, and it also never occurred to me that Liberace might be attracted to men. I suspect it did not occur to my aunts, either. Much like the docents interviewed at the now-defunct Liberace Museum in Las Vegas, I imagine my aunts' reluctance to discuss the topic even as they admired his high-heeled boots and marabou scarves. Even if there had been willingness to discuss that topic, "gay" did not exist in my vocabulary.

I do not remember ever hearing that word as a child, and because it was absent in my lexicon, I imagine it was even more acutely absent from my aunts' world. Gay, when I eventually heard it mentioned, was a high school insult or a whispered insinuation, never an orientation.

———

Likewise, as a little boy, Trav had lacked words to describe his experience at the American Boychoir School. There is reluctance even now to use the right words: rape, assault, abuse. These words make people squirm and flinch, so the phrasing softens to terms like molestation, fondling, and inappropriate contact. Still, these words present uncomfortable images, so we settle for even broader, more nondescript language. "That" is what happened.

"That" did happen to Trav.

It is no surprise that Liberace's rise in popularity coincided with the return of postwar veterans. Hardened, alcoholic, and shell-shocked, these soldiers lacked vocabulary, too. In a culture devoid of language for traumatic and emotional experiences, many men were reluctant to exhibit any sensitivity while existing in a world with fixed ideas of masculinity. For women of that era, Liberace performed with a level of public gentleness and glamor as he entertained. He preened live onstage, and then on television, and he asked women in the audience their opinion, as if it mattered. "Do you like this ring?" "Do you like this outfit?"

———

On one of our first dates, I brought Trav to a coworker's fund-raiser for Dignity, a group of gay Catholics. While I wanted to support the cause, I also wanted to watch Trav's reaction, hoping that his talk of tolerance would translate into action. That night, we represented a handful of straight couples in a full auditorium, and we watched the DC Cowboys dance troupe perform a campy and charged routine. The program included a dramatic monologue, interpretive ballet, and three men in Charlie's Angels drag. When a man performed a choreographed baton-twirling finale, I leaned in to my future husband. "What are you thinking?" I asked.

"Those batons would make fantastic weapons."

He passed the test.

———

At Chamblin Bookmine, I never found *Liberace Cooks!*, but in fairness, I never asked for assistance, either. I did manage to lose myself among the stacks because the interior was a wobbly maze of off-kilter aisles piled to the ceiling with old books. The flooring, uneven, dipped and buckled around each tight corner.

In many bookstores, aisles are neat and square. Not so at Chamblin Bookmine. The space weaves and twists. Books are stacked, as well as presented in traditional upright lines. Handwritten sticky notes direct the categories. My eye caught a biography of two flight attendants, and then a "What Ever Happened To" series from the 1960s. There was an entire room-sized section crammed with secondhand *Twilight* paperbacks.

I lost Trav within the first minute of entering the shop. Briefly, I panicked when I realized that all orientation was gone. Retracing my steps, I looked up at the ceiling to locate the perimeter, but given the height of the shelves, even the outer walls were impossible to isolate.

Ultimately, I sat down on a strip of musty-smelling brown carpet that covered a portion of the vast concrete floor, overwhelmed and suddenly aware that navigating sex abuse is like this disorienting bookstore experience. I leaned against the wooden shelf and flipped through a faded atlas. In a world filled with information, it is difficult to know which direction to take, and it is impossible to fix a solid position. Extending that metaphor, it is an often ugly, winding path where the best resources are concealed by millions of approaches, each citing endorsements from experts.

Distraction happens, and even in a mine full of words, it can be difficult to find the right ones.

CHAPTER TWENTY-TWO
The Power of Recollection

I n the most formative of little-boy years, in the care of a prestigious vocal academy, Trav suffered the stigma of being from a small town in northern Maine.

"Who would believe me?" he asked. "I was a scholarship kid."

"I believe you," I answered.

This is when we talked about the weird fluidity of memories.

The human brain rarely remembers details in a linear manner. Instead, the process becomes a series of associations, each prompting another association. A particular scent links to an event, and that event prompts an emotion. Two people can experience the same set of circumstances with two opposite perceptions, each convinced theirs is the correct interpretation.

Memory is tricky this way.

———

Trav and I arrived at coastal Georgia's Cumberland Island ferry with a cold hiking-day forecast, low 40s Fahrenheit. Trav seemed skeptical, but since island visitors are limited, and ferry reservations are accepted six months in advance, I was reluctant to divert from the plan.

"You will love it," I repeated, remembering the Cumberland Island of my early twenties.

My AmeriCorps team had bunked in a former servant quarters not far from the crumbling ruins of Dungeness, a mansion that was once a playground for the Carnegie family. As a volunteer, I explored those ruins while watching a family of wild horses frolic nearby. It was a short walk to miles of pristine, deserted, white-sand beaches.

I thought briefly of splurging on a stay at the island's only hotel, the antique-filled historic Greyfield Inn, originally built for Margaret Ricketson, the daughter of Thomas and Lucy Carnegie. However romantic and luxurious the space, even with meals and ferry fees included, the minimum stay of two nights was outside our budget. Given Trav's security parameters and unwillingness to wear a jacket for dinner, I also did not want to chance an incident.

Guests at the Greyfield Inn lived a world away from my AmeriCorps experience, but while volunteering on the island, I did find time to visit the First African Baptist Church, a tiny chapel made famous when John F. Kennedy, Jr., married Carolyn Bessette in the humble, worn, wooden space. At the time, when I posed for a photo to mimic the iconic hand-kissing moment, it was the closest I had ever come to touching a lifestyle of extreme wealth and privilege.

Cumberland Island was the most peaceful place I had ever experienced, I said to Trav over and over again throughout the years of our relationship, and I was excited to finally share it with him. As a volunteer, I had monitored sea turtles, watching scientists cut the heads off carcasses and plopping them in a bucket for examination in a strange little shack lined with shelves of meticulously numbered turtle shells.

"Sounds amazing," Trav deadpanned.

"No, seriously," I explained, noting that the shack was, as I remembered it, part of the Smithsonian Institution.

———

When I reviewed my paper journals from that time period, there was a flower pressed into the pages. My cursive was looser and loopier than it was later, and the words read happy. The project lasted a few weeks, but the impact held on for a lifetime.

This particular detour along Georgia's Gold Coast, I swore, would be a highlight.

I explained the details I had researched: the Carnegie connection, the ferry times, and the hiking trails. I also explained the details I remembered: pulling up baby tung trees and other nonnative species, replanting dune grass, the daily parade of wild horses, and swimming naked in the warm ocean water. This part of the trip would be the best, I insisted, trying to decide if it was better to hike the full loop or rent bicycles for the day.

When we arrived, it was, as with New Orleans, uncharacteristically cold. I stuffed sandwiches into a backpack while Trav watched the darkening, overcast sky.

"You will love it even if it rains a little," I assured him. "I know you will."

I imagined a day of hiking and fun facts shared by the rangers. I tucked in extra snacks and water, confident in my recollections, as Trav noted the chilly drops beginning to fall.

He had woken up early as a favor to me, and he did his best to remain un-grumpy. Surely, I thought, the rain would stop soon.

The ferry operated on an abbreviated schedule in February. Once island passengers disembark from the boat's morning run, they remain on the island for more than six hours. When I first booked the tickets, I worried six hours might not be enough time.

Memory works in funny ways, and especially so with childhood sexual abuse. Memories shift and burst, except instead of me leading Trav around island trails, soaked by the freezing rain and insisting the project site I had worked on twenty years ago must be nearby, it is Trav perceiving an instance of trauma as a felt sense, an instinct, or a quick and brutal flash of detail.

While my self-loathing is limited to backtracking through yet another slippery, wet, wooded path, Trav gets stuck in the self-loathing of wondering how the grotesquely outsized images in his head could possibly be real. Then, as details build and his certainty grows, he is left to wonder what horror he might recall next.

That is how memory works. It is distorting. It is ambiguous, except for when it is painfully acute.

———

The ferry ride was choppy, and the boat cabin nearly vacant. The last time I had ridden it, I leaned on the railing after arriving too late for a seat in the shoulder-to-shoulder crowd. With Trav sitting beside me in the empty space, I scanned for uniformed rangers or anyone who looked familiar and who might have been working twenty years ago.

We trudged off the boat with a half dozen others just as the iciest rain began to fall. Trav had packed two hats, and I asked to borrow one. With six hours to explore in a downpour, what seemed like barely enough time from a distance now felt like an eternity.

With conviction, I said, "This is the way," and chose a trail that dead-ended into a swampy field.

Seeing my dismay at the difference between the lush, green, coastal paradise I had described for decades and the colorless, freezing reality of our current trek, Trav tried to cheer me by admiring the Spanish-moss draped trees.

"Chiggers live there," I explained, remembering the tiny red biting bugs and cautioning him not to touch it.

"I was trying to find a bright side."

Eventually we found a path, and I talked again about the majestic wild horses.

The history of the Cumberland Island horses is debatable, and although legend places their origin as part of sixteenth-century Spanish settlement, experts agree that the more likely source is eighteenth-century British settlers. Between 100 and 200 feral horses roam the island, and the image of wild horses running at a full pace along the seashore would make the entire road trip worth the time spent.

As soon as we found those horses, I would be vindicated.

Approximately one hour into our wintry, wet, single-file march, I spotted two silhouettes in the distance.

"Shhh." I stopped, pointing to a clearing in the trees. I whispered, "See?"

To his credit, Trav got excited, too.

Slowly, not wanting to spook them, we tiptoed closer.

Like an Impressionist painting, what looked exquisite from a distance blurred on closer inspection. The two horses in the distance were, in clearer sight, neither majestic nor resplendent.

Instead, they were two emaciated creatures shivering in a field. I counted their ribs and noted their glassy eyes.

As Trav approached, these sad and lonely horses seemed too weak to resist the advance of strangers. They watched us as we watched them, and they stayed bony and motionless as we eventually walked past, so close that our arms could have brushed their fur.

We found Dungeness, too. Still a crumbling shambles, I experienced it this time in a now-icy downpour.

"Are you hungry?" I asked, and we sat down to eat soggy sandwiches.

After lunch, the worst of the wind and rain dissipated. It was still cold, but the sun improved our exploration. Eventually, we found a boardwalk that led to an observation station.

"I really think my team helped construct this boardwalk." I scanned the wood we stood upon. "Or," confused, I said, "something like it."

The hot days and cool nights I saw with clarity, but standing on planks that looked and felt familiar, I could not remember whether my team did the actual building, or I heard about the boardwalk from another team, or I read the detail in a report.

———

Trav and I managed to spend the day without talking about the Boychoir, but standing on that boardwalk with sudden and profound confusion, I understood the problems with old memories.

My projects on the island had been transformative twenty years earlier. I knew I had pounded boards somewhere, watched the sea turtles, pulled the nonnative and invasive species, driven a Jeep along sandy roads, and swum naked in the ocean on a summer night. I knew an engorged tick was once pulled from my shin.

But I could not remember where.

Or with whom.

Or any details I could reliably relay to Trav. I wanted him to feel proud when his wife pointed to the line of planks and said, "I did this," but I lacked precision of recall. My own mind felt foreign and my perceptions unreliable because I could not remember whether I had helped build this particular boardwalk or a similar boardwalk, or I was transferring details I had been told. Was the boardwalk a project I read about? Declined? Completed?

I could not remember with any level of accuracy, and I felt a strong, sympathetic pull toward Trav as we trudged off the observation deck and toward the beach trail.

My long-ago Cumberland Island experience had been only positive for me. Not just positive; it was all-consuming, and ranked among my top ten life experiences. Still, my brain could not summon details. I knew I felt joy and accomplishment, but I could not say for certain what month I had lived there. Spring? Summer? I would need to consult those paper journals again to make sure.

That is when I understood, gravely, a new level of trauma's complexity.

I tried to imagine the impact of negative experiences—an experience not just negative, but profoundly traumatic, shameful, and designed for the mind to protect with suppression and denial.

Then, in what felt like the quickest of moments, we saw them.

Six horses—strong and healthy—appeared on our periphery. We heard the rustle and thump of their approach before we saw their shiny, muscular bodies, but when we saw them—all shades of brown from latte to cocoa and blurred due to their pace—I jolted, feeling vindicated because my memory had not failed me. These were the horses I remembered, and what I knew to be true was quite real.

With speed and focus, these horses ran by us in a pack, intent and never wavering in direction. The horses moved in unison, with their manes flowing, and not two seconds later they had run across the trail, into the woods, and toward the ocean until the trail was empty again.

I looked at Trav to confirm that we did witness the horses, because if there were no footprints embedded in the wet, sandy path before us, I might have thought the scene was an illusion.

CHAPTER TWENTY-THREE
Low-Country Blues

The drive from Georgia to Charleston, South Carolina, ended with supper at Bowens Island restaurant. Since my last cramped and long-ago visit, the original graffiti-splashed, tight, cinder block establishment where the oyster roaster guy shoveled a pile onto the center of a newspaper-covered table and the beverage options were canned beer or tap water had morphed into a much larger, more open, friendlier, full-service water-view restaurant with a wood interior.

The large plastic bucket positioned between our chairs for shucked shells felt like a throwback to the old days, and I thought, *also very convenient*, as we worked our knives into the tight clusters of roasted oysters.

Shocked at the changes, I later learned the space had been rebuilt after a fire.

On the walk out, we paused to watch the orange-and-pink South Carolina sunset over the restaurant's metal roof. We had recovered from the frigid Cumberland Island day hike, and even found a broken piece of lightning whelk shell. Elaborate and striped, it had once been larger than Trav's fist, and it now rested on the dashboard.

Despite the bad-weather hiking situation, I asked Trav to trust me about Charleston food culture, and he agreed. Bowens Island was a good start.

————

The next morning we found Hominy Grill and stood in line with the weekend brunch crowd. A Charleston fixture, this restaurant had once served me well as a local, and I anticipated the same for the tourist experience.

Having opted for indoor seating even though the morning had started to warm up, we settled into the quaint, airy dining room. I knew I wanted the vile-sounding Charleston Nasty Biscuit with its fried chicken smothered in homemade sausage cream gravy, but I scanned the beverage menu and tried to decide between a straight-up Bloody Mary or a big cup of Planter's Punch made with Flor de Caña rum and orange and pineapple juice.

Then I stopped.

Trav had been sober for a year, and as a supportive partner, I tried to limit my own alcohol consumption in his presence.

"When you make a big deal about it," he had told me early on, "it feels more like a big deal."

"Okay," I said, and I had managed to give away the entirety of my wine stash over the past year. Trav hates the taste of gin, so I kept that bottle, but apart from the gin, some cognac in the freezer, and a few dusty mini-souvenir bottles of Caribbean rum I doubted we would ever open, our house was completely dry.

When Trav got the alcoholism diagnosis, we were both surprised, but as with childhood sexual abuse and its effects, we learned that alcoholism rarely resembles the common stereotypes of it. Trav never hit bottom. Always in control of his personal space, Trav rarely drank to excess.

Still, victims of sexual assault are three times more likely to suffer from depression, six times more likely to suffer from post-traumatic stress disorder, thirteen times more likely to abuse alcohol, twenty-six times more likely to abuse drugs, and four times more likely to contemplate suicide.[8]

Trav's alcohol problem developed when whiskey became a habit, a social crutch, and, eventually, a workplace necessity.

"It helps me do my job," Trav said of the whiskey shots he drank each night before stepping onstage and slipping the guitar strap over his shoulder.

More whiskey at his first break kept him mellow until he drank coffee at his second break. By then, he was sober and able to drive himself home.

As with every diagnosis, every twist, and every exhausting effort, Trav accepted the diagnosis as a challenge. When Vic said, "Alcoholism," Trav emptied those bottles in the same matter-of-fact way he had emptied the prescription sleeping pills.

---

8 *"Who Are the Victims?" RAINN (Rape, Abuse and Incest National Network), accessed October 2, 2015,* http://rainn.org.

My own experience with whiskey was much different. "I really think your body chemistry is such that you are probably one of those weird people who could try heroin once and not get addicted," Trav observed about my capacity to take or leave most recreational drugs.

My first real experience with whiskey, interestingly, began in Charleston. It culminated with the night I stripped on a Charleston bar top as part of a three-girl lineup. My friends and I secured sponsors for the evening, and the corner booth table at Big John's Tavern was topped with shots. We had our pick, and I moved toward the whiskey.

Since those were the days of the mini-bottles—a strange South Carolina rule for many years forbade bars from pouring liquor from large, standard-sized bottles—the liquor was uniformly strong.

With the jukebox turned up, I hopped onto the bar and found stripping surprisingly easy. Somewhere in the world exists a photo of me topless, wearing just jeans and cowboy boots, twirling my red bra above my head like a lariat. Thankfully, my face is obscured by a Foster's Ale sign. The wash of patrons below me that night were mostly good-ole-boy types wearing Top-Siders and Duck Club belts, or Citadel cadets released for the weekend.

Sometimes I wonder where that girl went.

"I was more audacious then," I note when old flames and old friends resurface, "but I am smarter now."

That is also how being married to a sexual abuse survivor feels sometimes—like there is a before and an after. Before I met Trav and after I met Trav. When I assign events to the two columns, my life is eminently better, saner, and smarter in the "after," but sometimes I'm nostalgic for the audacious "before."

———

So, while I hesitated over the Hominy Grill's beverage menu, Trav caught the hesitation.

"If you want a Bloody Mary," he said, "I think you should get one."

At first I brushed it off, knowing I would be happy with coffee, and then I saw a flicker of a familiar emotion in Trav's expression.

He, too, wished for some of the "before," and with this in mind, he squeezed my fingers.

"Please," he said. "I appreciate the solidarity, but I want us to feel normal."

"Well," I said, squeezing his fingers back, "this *is* 'Free Eat' day," and when the server arrived, I requested a Bloody Mary with my Charleston Nasty biscuit.

CHAPTER TWENTY-FOUR
Don't Ask, Don't Tell

harleston's Drayton Hall differs from the restored Magnolia Plantation down the road, and after we saw the empty square edifice, the edict requiring its preservation instead of restoration made sense. Drayton Hall's Palladian architecture remains minimally altered, and its bare space showcases details that would be easily lost in a meticulous, period-specific recreation.

After my AmeriCorps contract ended, I secured a West Ashley neighborhood apartment from an advertisement in the *Post and Courier* and paid the deposit and first month's rent in cash. I remember negotiating the terms from a truck stop pay phone on the way back from a Maine visit.

It was a period of independence, and South Carolina is where I developed my adult identity. For spouses of survivors, that is important. It is so easy to get consumed by a partner's healing process.

Of course, I visited Drayton Hall while living in Charleston. I admired the twin exterior staircases and the impact of the hollow interior space. Because it is situated on a river, one of the more common transportation routes, the back of the house was designed to receive guests arriving by boat and intended to be as impressive as the front, and I imagined the process of disembarking from the boat and seeing the majestic building.

Two sides. Equally imposing.

When Trav and I toured Drayton Hall as part of the road trip, I noticed many details I had overlooked when I visited there in my early twenties. Most interesting to me was not the intricate scrollwork I recalled from memory, but the smooth wooden door leading up to Drayton Hall's attic that I had never noticed. The docent drew our attention to the small, primitive square cut at the base of the door. This was, she said, to accommodate the family cat. The cat's name was Tom, and she said the preservation crew had discovered hundreds of rodent skeletons in the attic.

In our tour cluster of thirty visitors was a couple with an adolescent daughter confined to a special chair. She was nonverbal; her diagnosis likely included a palsy-type developmental disorder. In and out of a dozing state, she alternated between excitable spasms and guttural vocalizations.

Drayton Hall was built with three levels, and while two of the levels are moderately accessible, the family was asked to use the plantation's own wheelchair due to some awkward dimensions. The family had obviously called ahead to plan, but they did not anticipate how to get their daughter up the initial set of exterior stairs.

Trav watched the couple assess the steps, then he introduced himself and offered to help. Not only did he offer; his smile and body language exuded friendliness when he leaned in to grab a side of the chair. It was a genuine "let's do this together" attitude that felt neither false nor intrusive.

It is what he does. Trav extended his assistance while looking the parents in their eyes and asking, "What's your daughter's name?" in a way that felt both humanizing and validating.

Then, at the top of the steps, he moved aside and let them transfer their daughter on their own. When the tour was done, it was a repeat. He reappeared to help carry the girl back down to ground level.

And me? I fumbled. My contribution was to offer a compliment on their daughter's long, curly hair. I watched this family with their daughter who was in and out of consciousness and making guttural sounds. Both parents' faces seemed ashen and weary. The mother's eyes drooped, and the father's posture suggested resignation. Still, they both smiled through the tour.

As I watched Trav help the family lift their daughter's weight, I thought about the inherent respect in the process of wearing some issues, unashamed, on the outside.

The irony of touring an institution built by enslaved people did not go unnoticed. This is when the Boychoir parallels popped up in abundance, and again, childhood sexual abuse colored an otherwise happy day. Abhorrently, slavery happened in the United States. Abhorrently, child sexual abuse happens in the United States, too.

Drayton Hall does not shy away from its history, and its description uses people-first language. "Community of enslaved people" is the phrasing, and given the thorny, complicated issue, I found a level of honesty in the institution's word choice. In addition to the white Drayton family's history, promotional material gave equal attention to the Bowens family of enslaved people arriving from Barbados in the 1670s.

Drayton Hall is powerless to reverse centuries of slavery, but with the prominent recognition of the long-enslaved community as people, the organization demonstrates, at a minimum, an effort to turn a national horror into a teaching moment.

I wish all institutions with child sexual abuse in their history would do the same.

CHAPTER TWENTY-FIVE
Moving Through Rowland

T rav's full, honest, in-depth disclosure happened in this order: me, his parents, and his best friend, Higgins. Higgins is not his real name, but the designation will likely amuse him because he appreciates 1980s television programming as much as Trav. Higgins works as a high-ranking military officer who served tours of combat duty in both Iraq and Afghanistan. He earned recognition and many medals for this military service, and because he does not ever discuss the details of his assignments, I assume Higgins is an international spy. Like any effective spy, Higgins denies being a spy, and I wink in solidarity.

Because Higgins and his family were stationed in North Carolina at the time of our road trip, we planned a visit to reconnect. This reunion put us on Highway 301, rambling north toward Fayetteville.

Higgins is a thoughtful, pragmatic, witty, and gentle man. Before Higgins launched his career as a spy, he and Trav spent their teenage years driving circles around Houlton, Maine's downtown loop, eating fries from McDonald's, longing for female attention, and listening to very loud music. Having studied the nuances of front men like Axl Rose from Guns N' Roses and Skid Row's Sebastian Bach, Trav and Higgins also formed a high school heavy metal band.

Trav described their biggest gig performing on stage during a demolition derby at a Fourth of July agricultural fair, where a handful of the gray-headed derby crowd lingering on the fringes of the muddy track turned their lawn chairs to face the small stage.

At the time, my husband's bright red curls were cut into a three-dimensional mullet of exceptional length, height, and girth. Trav details the hours spent slicing and bleaching his jeans and tying his rayon paisley blouse into a Daisy Duke-style knot to better feature his abdominal muscles. Higgins chose a shirtless vest, cowboy boots, and a peace medallion necklace.

It was, Trav explained with dry observational humor and flawless hindsight, an exercise in knowing your audience.

After graduating high school and leaving our hometown, they remained friends, and Higgins has been a constant presence in Trav's life, throughout adolescence and now into middle age.

Higgins had endured many pained excursions with Trav as his awkward wingman, neither of them particularly adept at wooing women. Higgins had flown to Maine for a birthday canoe trip surprise, spent a night battling a Lake Champlain storm beside Trav in a sailboat, stood beside him as his best man, and hosted Trav and me for an entire month in his tropical island apartment.

Trav swam with Higgins during many teenage summer afternoons at a hometown lake, and when visiting their parents now as men, they still make time for this ritual. Trav returned from one of those lake swims and said, as a casual afterthought in the way a person might mention the weather during a change in season, "I told Higgins."

It was so nonchalant, I nearly missed it. "Everything?"

Trav nodded.

When I asked how Higgins had responded, Trav still underplayed the bravery of his disclosure.

"He was cool."

I never doubted it.

———

At Higgins's wedding rehearsal dinner, Trav met Higgins's wartime buddies. Tall or jacked with muscles (sometimes both), these men filled the space with a level of bold and friendly masculine swagger. Although Trav smiled through the event, shaking hands and showing his most welcoming presence, he confessed his insecurities as we left the party.

"All of his friends are so cool," he sighed. "They carry weapons."

Given the way childhood sexual abuse can profoundly affect the perception of masculinity, I thought about that observation for a few moments before I spoke.

"I think there are two primary hetero male fantasies," I said. "The hero and the rock star." I patted his leg. "Just wait until tomorrow."

We had met a crew of heroes that night, but at the next day's wedding, while Trav performed the music, I overheard Higgins's friends lamenting to each other near the edge of Trav's stage with sincere envy.

"Man, I wish I could play the guitar like that."

———

The only time I have ever directed anger at Higgins happened after a 3:00 A.M. telephone wakeup. Because of time zone differences, Trav and Higgins tend to call each other at odd hours. During one of these calls, they ran down a list of approximately 100 Chuck Norris one-liners.

"Chuck Norris doesn't sleep," Trav said in a voice that seemed to scream from the office below our bedroom. "He waits."

He paused for Higgins to add the next one-liner, and whatever Chuck Norris did on the other end of the line caused more shrieking, hysterical laughter in a straight auditory path to my sleeping ears.

"Chuck Norris wasn't born," Trav shouted, at that point choking laughs before the punch line. "He kicked his way out of the womb."

I lost count of the jokes, but at some point during the exchange I pushed back the blankets and stomped to the top of the stairs. Trav's voice stopped midsentence when he heard my footsteps and saw my shadow extend into his peripheral view. We both felt the energy shift, and I do not recall the exact words I used to silence the shrieking Chuck Norris, but in the morning Trav apologized. Higgins did, too.

"I never saw rage like that from you before," Trav observed, clearly impressed. "It was like you were channeling the wrath of God."

———

When my first essay appeared in the *Atlantic*, it was the note from Higgins that moved me to tears.

"Your husband is a much braver man than me," he wrote.

Given the nature of Higgins's profession, the longstanding friendship, and Trav's absolute respect for the integrity of his friend's opinion, those words rank among the most powerful responses to that essay.

I cannot overstate the importance of having Higgins as part of Trav's support system, and I imagine it is similar for any male survivor—a strong, rugged, smart friend with integrity and a vocation that no outsider would ever consider weak. Higgins carries weapons. He strategizes on missions. I have not asked, but I suspect he's probably killed people.

Higgins himself likely has to deal with his own variety of war-related post-traumatic stress disorder, and having this man in Trav's corner—this man who "gets" it—has been instrumental in Trav's healing.

———

Trav dialed his best friend's telephone number from the van to arrange an arrival time.

"Yo, Shit Feet," he said, followed by a loud belch.

I do not understand this method of Trav and Higgins's communication, so I tuned out the dialogue and educated myself on the dusty little town of Rowland, a town my GPS said we were quickly approaching, and a town that reminded me powerfully of a dozen little towns in northern Maine.

Situated in Robeson County, Rowland bills itself as "Home of a Thousand Friends." This motto is a nod to Rowland's approximately 1,000 full-time residents. According to the town website, 6,000 people pass through Rowland every day on their way to or from somewhere else.

The town website told me the community of Rowland originally developed from a network of farming communities and was established as a result of new railroads being built as supply routes between Wilson,

North Carolina, and Florence, South Carolina, known as the "Wilson Shortcut."

Rowland was incorporated in 1889 and Colonel Alfred Rowland, the town's namesake, died on August 2, 1898. Since I was born on August 2 seventy-five years later, this felt significant.

As we meandered through the little town, a town with an elaborately bricked and vacant-storefront main street that resembled our own hometown's elaborately bricked and vacant-storefront main street, I thought of all the teenagers who might be shooting the downtown loop in the same way Trav and Higgins had done so frequently as young men.

As stated previously, one in four women and one in six men is sexually abused as a child. Conservatively speaking, if half the Rowland population is male, at least eighty-three of Rowland's 1,000 friendly faces have likely experienced male childhood sexual abuse.[9]

I wondered about those eighty-three men, assigning them jobs as shop owners, farmers, office workers, salesmen, athletes, students, and retirees. As a game, I tried to quickly think of eighty-three separate professions to match up to the eighty-three statistical victims.

Childhood sexual abuse pops up in weird ways, and it is a numbers game I often play. When I hear population information or death tolls, I quickly estimate the male head count and then divide that number by six.

If six men attend a meeting, I wonder which one might have been hurt. When I look at my class rosters, I do a count, too. At the water park with my sister's children, I counted every sixth boy who ran up

---

9 *Obviously, I am not suggesting that eighty-three male residents of Rowland, North Carolina, have, in fact, experienced childhood sexual abuse. I use Rowland's population of approximately 1,000 residents as numerical context.*

the stairs with an inner tube. It is another hidden effect of childhood sexual abuse for partners like me.

I scan photographs and wonder with an involuntary reflex, "You? You? Or you?"

By the time I mentally ticked off all eighty-three imaginary professions in my brain, Trav had ended the conversation with Higgins, and we were well past Rowland.

———

One of the kindest things Higgins has done throughout this process is to not treat Trav as if he is a vampire. There is actually a myth as it relates to child sexual abuse, called "vampire syndrome." Because many child sex offenders were abused themselves, it is a common perception that *all* victims will become abusers, similar to the notion that those bitten by vampires are destined to become vampires themselves.

Sex offenders are more likely to have been abused themselves; this is true. But, while the math works in one direction, it absolutely does not compute both ways.

Approximately 500,000 children will be sexually abused in the United States each year.[10] If the vampire syndrome were true, assuming a modest one to one victim ratio that doubles annually, within ten years the United States would be a nation composed primarily of sex offenders. Statistically, this is impossible. Still, the myth persists.

Most victims will never commit sexual violence.

10 *"Child Sexual Abuse Facts," The Children's Assessment Center, Houston, TX. Accessed February 17, 2016, http://cachouston.org.*

———

The visit with Higgins and his family led to one of the best souvenir photos of the trip. Trav is standing in the living room with his arms outstretched and holding each of Higgins's young sons—for these purposes, Zeus and Apollo—upside down by an ankle.

Kids adore Trav, and both Zeus and Apollo treat him like a large, impenetrable human jungle gym. The Higgins boys climbed him, rushed his legs, touched his tattooed arms, and patted his bald head.

"I have never had feelings like *that*," Trav once told me, and I felt sad and angry that he needed to say those words aloud or that anyone might ever doubt his character, especially around children.

Still perceptions are difficult to change.

Watching Trav hoist two giggling little boys above his head by their ankles while Higgins and his wife sat relaxed on the couch made me realize that while perceptions are often slow to change, this is how perceptions *do* change—one trusted person at a time.

Rather than discuss child sexual abuse during the visit, we talked about musician Gram Parsons. Upon Gram Parsons's death, in a ceremony more fitting for them than for Parsons's family, his friends stole the body and set it on fire at Joshua Tree National Forest.

In a tone that I am never quite sure is serious, Trav reminded me of my promise to do something similar. I explained to Higgins that I actually looked up the legal consequences if we did, in fact, drag Trav's burning corpse into a field or set it adrift on the water. Turns out it is not so bad. As I understood it, desecration of a corpse in Maine would be considered a misdemeanor, with a $500 fine.

Higgins just shook his head as though Trav's outrageousness were somehow antithetical to his own instincts, forgetting that in addition to wearing a shirtless vest and peace medallion for a heavy metal concert at an agricultural fair, he once woke me from a dead sleep after volleying some version of "Chuck Norris sheds his skin twice a year."

Trav insisted on a funeral pyre, and he made us both promise.

"I'd be okay if you used accelerants," he assured us.

CHAPTER TWENTY-SIX
Genetic Trash

"You would be fantastic parents." This comes from all manner of well-meaning people, and Trav and I generally nod in equal parts agreement and vanity. Agreement and vanity, because we, too, believe we would excel at anything we really tried to do. Fantasy contenders include international espionage, floral design, long-haul trucking, high-priced escorting—each of these scenarios being as random and strange to us as producing a child.

Part of the assessment is fair. In our years together, we have structured a life like teenagers. We sleep late and are terrible money savers. Our house is a shrine to books and music, and my first-edition Dorothy Parkers line the same low shelves as his Dick Curless vinyl albums. Laundry is piled on the guest room bed, and dirty dishes are piled in the kitchen sink. We recite takeout menus by heart, and the litter box is usually full.

Part of the assessment, though, is unintentionally cruel. Trav and I thought we would eventually have children—not because either of us had a particular yearning to be parents, but because we were too preoccupied to use birth control. If it happened, we reasoned, it happened. "No big deal," we thought. We would roll with it.

Plus, we had bigger health issues to worry about.

When we saw the line on the stick, Trav's "holy shit" preceded a celebratory dinner we could not afford. I clinked my wine glass, a final hurrah for me, over seared rare tuna and thought of Kinky Friedman's campaign slogan during his run for Texas governor: "How hard could it be?" The next day, when there was no longer a line on a second and then a third stick, Trav asked, "Do you want to have a baby?"

"I don't know," I said, meaning it. "Do you?"

We had half-assed our way for so long, focusing on the Boychoir effects, it did not occur to us to take an active role. Or that something might be wrong with my body. Or his body. Or that a baby conceived by two people with diagnosed disorders might be a bad idea. Or that raising a child while coping with the overwhelming repercussions of childhood sexual abuse might be a bad idea, too.

Once again, childhood sex abuse was coloring our life decisions.

———

After six more cycles of positive pregnancy tests that eventually turned negative, I sought a professional opinion, and the doctor herself asked loaded questions.

"How long have you been trying to conceive?"

There was no simple timeline for our situation.

"Never," I answered. "But maybe five years?"

After a series of tests, the phrase she used in her office was "genetic overlap." Given our shared hometown, Trav's reaction mirrored mine, and for a moment, both of us felt sick.

The doctor sketched balanced and unbalanced chromosomes on a piece of scrap paper, and she explained chemical pregnancies. I do get pregnant, but I do not stay pregnant for more than a couple of weeks.

"So we're not cousins," I confirmed.

Trav's face showed relief. "Just genetic trash?"

———

"It is unlikely you will carry a baby to term," the doctor said.

"So what now?" I asked.

She leaned back and asked if I wanted to have a child. I told her I did not think so.

"Then go live your life."

Oh, that.

It felt so simple in concept, but the antagonist in me said, "No."

"We'll adopt," I thought, walking down the medical center stairs, already fixated on the research process. International adoption, I learned, gave the most options, but it was pricey and forced us to confront our prejudices. Did we want an Asian baby? Hispanic? Indian? African? Chinese babies were the most expensive, but gender relinquishment seemed like a safer bet than the high rates of fetal alcohol syndrome cited at orphanages in other countries. The Central American programs felt like a bargain, but then stories of corruption leaked out. We could get a middle schooler in the United States foster care system for free.

I assembled adoption materials but deferred attending orientation sessions at least a dozen times in favor of movies, diner breakfasts, and the hair stylist. We took a trip to Florida, and then another to Hawaii. One morning, Trav gestured toward my dusty pile of adoption information.

"These kids deserve parents who will go through hell to get them." He paused. "I don't think that is us."

He was right. During one particular infertility test while waiting on the examination table and wearing a paper drape, I studied the wall with a corkboard full of baby photos—ugly babies, objectively cute babies—a smiling, scowling, smirking range of faces. I scanned them and felt nothing. Not a twang or a stirring or the longing my friends often described. "I always knew I wanted to be a parent" existed nowhere in my vocabulary. I always knew I wanted to write words. And to travel. Trav always knew he wanted to make music. We both knew, on the same primal level, we always wanted to eat good food and live in Maine.

We were committed to managing the demons in Trav's head, the panic surrounding mine, and the idea of bringing a third person into an already fraught existence seemed fundamentally selfish and cruel.

Maybe without the Boychoir specter? It is impossible to know.

———

"I always knew I wanted kids," my sister once told me with honest conviction, and I believe her. When I watch my niece grow tall and precocious, with eyeglasses and cheekbones that mimic mine, or my nephews scramble from room to room, I tell my sister she is a fantastic parent. Not that she *would be,* in some other fantasy existence like a rocket scientist or international spy or high-priced escort, but that she *is.*

Present tense.

Semantics again.

When babies cry, my sister knows what to do. She wakes up early, and she feeds them. My reaction to fluids is to hold the child at arm's length, while my sister draws them closer. She brushes their hair and reads aloud. More important than this, she tackles the daily tasks. The routine, the spoiled milk. Toilet training and dirty feet. She hollers, too.

I swoop in and spin magic. My sister corrals them, and I dress them up in costumes. "Sure," I once said at the candy store, passing out baskets. "Fill it up."

When my sister first gave birth, I stood in the delivery room with her. Afterward, when the rest of the family left the hospital, I took the overnight shift, on guard like a German Shepherd while my sister tried to sleep. In the early-morning hours, I wanted to hold the baby overhead, Kunta Kinte-style, and whisper Alex Haley's words as we watched the dawn: "The only thing greater than you."

I never once felt like changing a diaper.

When my sister had her second baby, I was there to brace her leg and then soon after rocked a little peanut baby in my arms in the early morning hours. This happened for baby number three, too, with me staring at the wonder of him.

Each time I smelled their warm, new little heads and whispered that their entire lives—every single moment—were starting right now.

Trav feels the same love, but his love is coupled with a harsh, protective instinct. Children make him nervous, not because of any vampire-syndrome fears, but because children are fundamentally vulnerable and weak.

"The responsibility is too much."

For me, it is the daily grind. For Trav, it is the weight of having more people to protect.

———

Our nephews love to scale Trav's rock-solid frame as much as the Higgins boys. "Little monkeys!" Trav will holler, prepared to chase. This delights them, and Trav's engagement delights me because I know it is not intuitive.

In what has become tradition, the two of us offer a growling, collaborative bear hug when we say good-bye, and it makes the kids laugh hard.

Trav told of a recent visit with pride. "And he squealed, 'That's my uncle!' when he saw me."

It feels good to be involved in the kids' lives. It feels good, and what's also true is that the shadow of childhood sexual abuse settles hard. In an effort to be constantly above suspicion, Trav asks me to stay nearby when the kids are present.

"That's silly," I want to say. It is a sentiment Trav's friends and family share, and I want to dismiss his request, but to Trav, in his constant state of hypervigilance, it is the opposite of silly.

To Trav, it is smart policy.

Trav once hesitated before helping a nephew straighten a pair of badly twisted pants. Only after seeing me across the lawn did he relax and assist.

"Oh, buddy, I understand," he told our nephew, with me never leaving his view. Our nephew wiggled with impatience as Trav pulled the pants comfortably up and over the boy's diaper and then fist-bumped the baby's hand in solidarity.

While I folded the same pants later, fresh from the laundry basket, this nephew pointed at me.

"Mama," he said with his little finger extended.

"You would make such fantastic parents," I imagined him saying, and it was too hard to explain that no, we would not. Our enthusiasm, our patience, our energy, our compassion, and our genuine interest—those are qualities that make us a fantastic aunt and uncle. Those are the qualities that make it bearable to deal with childhood sexual abuse in a manner that does not completely exhaust us and grind us both into sand.

But I underestimated him. I realized my nephew was not trying to say that he wanted me as his mama. He was, instead, confused and struggling for the right phrase. He pointed at me again and repeated his word for mother. Then, perplexed, he remembered his word for grandmother.

He lacked the language, but his arms flapped as he desperately tried to communicate. I put down the pants I had just folded.

No longer confused, I understood precisely his intentions.

"Auntie," I said, touching my chest and making eye contact.

He smiled, then he nodded, and he repeated an approximation of "Auntie" and pointed back at me. Then he rushed in for a big, full-body hug.

"Auntie," he repeated, "Auntie, Auntie, Auntie," as he snuggled into my neck.

Yes, "Auntie." That is exactly the right word.

———

Although sometimes I revisit the topic just to make sure, Trav is quick to reassure me. We talked about the decision to have kids over crepes with strawberries and hazelnut spread at Betsy's, a small Southern Pines café not far from the Higginses' house. Part by choice and part by circumstance, raising children is not an option for us.

A family with two babies waited for a table. I watched the family and thought about how different our own world might look.

For a moment I felt sad, as if I had been cheated out of one of life's most profound experiences. Then I watched Trav finish the last bite of his sweet crepe, and thought about how some people never get to feel a love like Trav's. Some people never receive a hug from a happy niece or nephew. Some people never, not for a single moment, get to linger over crepes in a sweet little restaurant.

Given our set of circumstances, "Auntie" felt as good as "Mama" ever could.

CHAPTER TWENTY-SEVEN
Name-Dropping DC Two-Step

The return stop in Washington, DC, included a dinner party hosted by old friends with Julia Child's coq au vin recipe, predinner cocktails, bottles of rich red wine, hilarious conversation, and strawberries macerated in maraschino liqueur. A five-fruit pie, biscotti, Chartreuse, and samples from our hosts' extensive collection of unusual alcohol completed the menu. Trav cheerfully offered to be the designated driver, and the next morning I squinted from under the covers.

It seemed I had developed a flu bug.

"You do not have the flu," Trav pointed out, handing me ibuprofen and bottled water with instructions to drink.

As I waited for the world to collapse inside my throbbing head, Trav proceeded to alternately blame the victim and rub my back while I disparaged our friends. It was clear they hated me and harbored a secret death wish for me. There had been six of us seated around that dinner table, and I could no longer trust any of them.

When the sunlight grew less intense, and my belly more steady, Trav indulged my desire to recreate our first-date walk through the National Mall.

The city was crowded with tourists, and the street traffic was tight. At the intersection near Union Station, I flashed on the first time I had an anxiety attack in front of another person. That person was Trav.

I was hyperventilating in the Union Station parking garage because Dr. Maya Angelou had invited me to her holiday party, and, after watching a dozen guests walk past the car in their designer gowns, I was so very ashamed that my own dress cost thirty dollars at Sears.

It was a dark-green dress, floor length. When I saw it on the rack, I thought the matching bolero jacket's satin lapels were elegant. It was a grown-up dress to wear with grown-up shoes to a grown-up party.

And then, in that parking garage with Maya Angelou's fancy printed invitation in my hand, those lapels had grown dull, and I could not breathe.

"Hey," Trav whispered as he rubbed my neck, now pushed between my knees in an attempt to not vomit.

I thought about his tuxedo on loan from the Air Force, and I thought about how that holiday party was the last time Trav ever wore a full tux. What struck me most was not that he showed kindness in the wake of my panic, or that he agreed to escort me to that party, or how he reassured me in the car after seeing those more elegant women glide past with "It takes those women out there *thousands* of dollars to look good," and then, when I twisted to see his face, "Do you know how proud I am that you can do it *even better* for thirty bucks at Sears?"

What struck me most was the timing.

This party was the one where Dr. Maya Angelou greeted me at the door and said, with such sincerity in her distinct voice, that she was so proud of the work I did for the homeless organization. This party also happened early in my relationship with Trav, well before any inklings of childhood sexual abuse had surfaced.

———

By the time Trav found on-street parking near the Lincoln Memorial, I had pieced together a more thorough timeline. It was Trav who rubbed *my* back during that first crippling panic attack in the car. He sent *me* to grad school with an encouragement card and then talked me through those first horrible days. Trav stood up and cheered when I received my diploma. The flutter of these snapshots in my head, instance after instance of Trav caring for me, was unending.

———

On another drive, earlier in our marriage, we stopped for supper at a country joint with phonetic menu spellings like "aigs" and "maters" and servers wearing denim overall uniforms. When, mid-conversation, just after our food arrived, the restaurant walls began to spin and my arms went as dull and immobile as sandbags, Trav keyed into yet another panic attack.

He did not flinch when I lost the ability to inhale properly, and he knew exactly where to find the pills in my purse. Without any tone of drama or alarm, Trav kept talking while I sweated through my shirt. Trying to remain conscious as the room grew blurry, I felt his hands rubbing my fingers as his garbled voice echoed as if through some distant tunnel.

Five minutes later, with my body exhausted and devoid of all color, Trav encouraged me to eat some food.

"Let's get your blood sugar level up," he said while cutting into his own meal as if watching his wife's restaurant freak-out was the most normal experience in the world.

———

Years ago, Trav found my medication at that country restaurant when my arms went numb. Trav sends funny text messages to make me laugh, and he followed the ambulance where I held the hand of a close friend just before she died.

Just this morning in DC after the reunion party, Trav handed me water to ease the effects of my overindulgence. He parked the van in the type of city traffic he loathes so we could again sit on the Lincoln Memorial steps.

———

It was Trav who tracked down a mint-condition copy of Henry Miller's *On Turning Eighty,* number 10 of 200 printed as a 1972 chapbook, each one signed by the author, for my last birthday.

"I don't care if it devalues the book," Trav told me when I read his inscription inside the cover. "Years from now, when we're dead, I want the person who finds this copy to know there was a man named Travis who loved his wife more than anything else."

That it was Henry Miller, an author banned for his explicit sexual depictions, did not escape me. Miller quotes Rabelais in the text: "For all your ills, I give you laughter." That adage did not escape me either.

What he offered me seemed—suddenly and acutely—so disproportionately wonderful compared to any of his issues.

There is a moment when a thunderstorm rolls in on a hot day, and in the span of five minutes, right after the worst of the rain, the sun begins to emerge again, the energy shifts, and in that instant the world is greener and refreshed. Trav's issues seemed small in comparison to the extreme level of comfort he added to my life, and I could only focus on yet another vivid, clear recollection.

We had attended a summer wedding, high up on a mountain; I wore a pink flowered sundress, and my skin had a healthy bronze tone. Trav said I looked very pretty with my hair pulled up and my rhinestone eyeglasses sparkling. Many friendly and interesting people gathered for the ceremony, and while Trav sang the welcome music and processional, another band had been hired for the reception.

Because Trav is a musician, I can count on my hands the number of Saturday nights we have spent together, so it was especially meaningful when I set my plate of wedding pie on a side table and had a slow dance with my husband on a Saturday night. I had not danced with Trav in a decade, and while neither of us are dancers, we fake a two-step with flair.

A local function band played a version of The Byrds covering Bob Dylan, and we slowed down our two-step. Emotionally exhausted from another rough patch, I rested my head on Trav's shoulder.

"Why wouldn't I want you?" he sincerely asked. "You are smart. You are funny. And you are so beautiful." He touched my neck in the softest, loveliest gesture. "And I love you so fucking much."

I needed to remember that moment on the wedding reception dance floor more often. I needed to remember that in moments of panic, it is

Trav's hands that steady me. I needed to remember that when broken down into its most basic form, nothing is as complicated as it might seem. It's all just spinning around on a dance floor, slow-slow-side-side, and I can always put my head on Trav's shoulder. I need to remember how much I love his pine-and-wood-fire smell, and how I would recognize it anywhere.

———

We walked to the steps of the Lincoln Memorial, but the crowd of camera-toting people seemed overwhelming, and neither of us felt like pushing our way past the slowly moving tourists.

"Hey," I said, touching his arm. "I know this great place for pie."

CHAPTER TWENTY-EIGHT
Home

Home. It is a loaded word, and I thought about the concept as we dodged the sleet en route to New Hampshire. We had chatted throughout our time in Washington, DC, had pie, this time at Dangerously Delicious, and with a whole pecan pie packed to go in the van, we hit the Massachusetts border before realizing we had talked our way well past New Jersey.

Huh, I thought, letting the magnitude of it sink in.

When we saw the Portsmouth highway sign, we were hungry again, and it was a slippery walk from the van to the parking lot to the sidewalk to the warm, weird Friendly Toast vestibule. Years ago Trav fell very quickly in love with a Friendly Toast server who accidentally poured hot coffee over her brightly tattooed arm without flinching.

"Baller," he said, impressed.

The Friendly Toast walls are decorated in decades' worth of vintage kitsch, and the menu has many favorites, but I almost always order the Damned Good Grilled Cheese because of its thick-cut cheddar garlic bread slices and the strawberry jalapeño jam for dipping.

When our coffee arrived, served in retro Thermo Serv-esque plastic mugs with a burlap pattern, Trav spilled some on his jeans and swore softly. I mentioned the tattooed server who had once impressed him by not flinching with the same hot coffee. There was, I said, no way I could endure hot coffee on my skin without crying.

"It is okay if you can't withstand extreme pain," he answered. "You wear an updo like a boss."

It was an earnest compliment.

———

After lunch we sat back in the van, one hour away from our house, and I was back to thinking about home during that last, final stretch of highway while the windshield wipers slapped in time to the radio.

Trav indulged my love of Leonard Cohen on this portion of the drive, and we talked about Alan Light's *The Holy or the Broken*, a book he had chosen for me because of my love for Cohen's voice. The book detailed the ascent of the song "Hallelujah," and although we disagreed about the impact of Leonard Cohen as a musician, we agreed about that particular song.

"'Hallelujah' is transcendent, Shonna," he said as we crossed the border into Maine. "Anything else is just another love song."

———

We could have made Nashville work, as there is no denying the abundance of music businesses and opportunity there. New Orleans, too, possesses enough outsider appeal for us both to enjoy. Less so Alabama, but in fairness, our trip through that state was a breeze. If it could inspire Emmylou Harris, as well as a standard of mental healthcare that is now replicated throughout the country, then why not Shonna and Travis Humphrey? That one pivotal, angry night in the musty-smelling Panama City Beach hotel and then the subsequent nights on the upgraded hotel's balcony, watching the dolphin pod and eating deli cheese from a plastic bag? That is a place I would love to return to but could probably never replicate in significance.

As I ticked off the places we'd traveled, from the dark corners of the Chamblin Bookmine to the vast, wide-open beaches on Cumberland Island to the cluttered voodoo shop where I received the voodoo lady's emphatic endorsement, I thought of how far we had progressed as a couple, and about the concept of home.

My ancestors left Scotland for Nova Scotia, and then slowly worked their way to northern Maine. Maine was home for both of us, deeply and irrevocably ingrained into our cultural and genetic being.

None of the places we had traveled to in the past few weeks was Maine, and as much as home is people, for us home is also this monosyllabic state with thick pine forests where the blackflies drive the summertime moose into the roadways at dusk, necessitating the "Danger: Moose Crossing" signs that punctuate the highway with a real and foreboding purpose. Maine is the waves slamming against the rocks surrounding Portland Head Light when the sky and water take on the same shade of color—blue on blue in the sun, and gray on gray under the clouds. It is the early-fall walk through the farmer's market at Deering Oaks Park, redolent with pumpkin, native plums, and apple cider. Home is the library's stone building within walking distance of our house and the librarians who know us by name. Trav's family house, at one time the site of his grandfather's used car lot, has welcomed visitors from his father's music store for decades.

Like our marriage, it is only during the bleakest, darkest winter storms that I want to flee, when other geographic corners and other people seem brighter, sunnier, and happier.

Brighter and sunnier, maybe, but—I correct my thoughts—not happier.

I was not happier when I lived in Charleston, or Washington, DC, or any of the places I had lived before meeting my husband. So, I stay. Even, and maybe especially, during the storming, ugly, and hopeless times.

Childhood sexual abuse is just one thing that happened to my husband.

Like those frigid, lonely winter months that do not define my home state and are not the whole of Maine, childhood sexual abuse is not the sum of him or our relationship.

It is easy—so very easy—to lose all perspective in this regard.

Rather than a geographic region, Trav is my home.

———

It was morning, barely, after our first night back. I heard Trav's steps on the stairs, and then his attempt to quietly twist the bedroom doorknob. I had forgotten to turn on the fan, so he clicked it to the highest setting. He adjusted the dark blanket that drapes over the window blinds.

Darkness and white noise are important, and I focused on the fan's soothing sound while Trav pulled back the covers and settled in.

By now, he had taken his list of medications. He had exercised, and he had meditated. I snuggled back into sleep after saying a quick and silent prayer that this night would be a peaceful one. As always, I hope the night moves quickly.

It was not, and it did not.

Two hours later, my husband thrashed himself upright into a sitting position, screaming "NO!" At this moment, the adrenaline in my own body surged, and I did a quick assessment while Trav panted.

"Shhh," I whispered, carefully touching his sweaty arm. He flinched at this touch, but as always, his shoulders relaxed when he heard my voice. "You're okay."

I repeated a mantra I could, literally, now repeat in my sleep. "You're okay. You're okay."

Because his breathing was ragged and uneven, I added "Take a breath, Trav" to the chant.

He did, and then he took another. In less than a minute his head was back on his pillow, and in two minutes he began to snore softly.

The clock blinked 4:15 A.M., and while my hand still rested on my husband's arm, the usual math happened.

I could try to sleep for a couple more hours, or I could start my day. When I moved my hand, Trav shifted, so I replaced my hand quickly, trying to stay as motionless as possible until he reached a deep level of sleep.

While I waited, I thought about how the list of physical aspects in our home had not changed because of the road trip. The basement still needed a full mold remediation, and the workers planned to arrive that afternoon. My broken toe still ached when I wiggled it. The night felt just as long, and I still mopped up the dirt tracked in from the rock salt used to melt the ice on our rotting deck.

The energy, however, had shifted significantly.

Instead of focusing solely on the heavy urine tang from where the cat had soaked our guest room bed in protest of our absence, I knew the mattress pad had a plastic lining, and I could wash it easily. Moreover, our house would soon smell like the box of Creole and Gullah spices we had ordered while on the road and that were waiting at the post office, ready to melt into the nutty brown roux I was planning to perfect.

Soon our dog—still wiggly and puppy-like—would be back and bouncing on the couch. I would share the special-ordered pralines and moon pies with my coworkers. I had purchased voodoo candles for the ladies in my writing group, and I looked forward to bringing the enormous souvenir seashells to my sister's children. Although we never found a St. Michael medal on the trip, I knew where to order one.

The external trappings were identical to what they had been before, but rather than depressed, I felt energized and hopeful.

From my spot in bed, I could see that when Trav had spread the thick, dark blanket over the window blinds, he left a sliver of window visible to me. It was in no way the bright, welcoming sunshine wakeup I craved, but it was, I noticed, another gesture in my direction.

I watched that sliver of window for the next hour as the inky darkness faded to a slightly lighter shade. Blue sky would take a few more hours to appear, but I could distinguish a clear difference in color tone.

Closing my eyes, I wondered what terrifying scene had played out in Trav's mind on this first night back, and I hoped that when he woke up to begin his new day, he would not remember. Again, that is the beauty of his current medication regimen. The night terrors happen, but he rarely remembers the details.

It is, I suppose, a blessing.

"I am glad we have the problems we do." Trav says this often as the voice of reason and hope. I admire his pragmatism. It is one reason I love him so damned much.

"You didn't choose weak," a friend observed after first meeting Trav. She was right.

That is why, when people ask about my passion for the issue of childhood sexual abuse, its young and old victims, and the people who love them—I do not want to be weak, either. I want my husband to know that, unlike him, I cannot bench-press hundreds of pounds. My biceps are tiny compared to his, but I need Trav to know that I am not weak, either.

I wish the American Boychoir School president would write a note that says, "I am so sorry for what happened to you, and I am committed to making sure all the victims are cared for. How can the school help you heal?"

I wish a lot of things.

Trav suffers from post-traumatic stress disorder and will likely manage symptoms in some way until he dies. Anxiety affects me more than most people know. Also true: I am the wife of a beautiful, strong, talented man, and it is my honor and privilege to help him live his best life.

This radical acceptance is, in a way, a riff on the serenity prayer.

Instead of focusing on the negatives, I listed the positives.

"We're going to be okay" topped the list.

At that moment in bed, when I finally moved my hand from Trav's arm, it was not aspirational thinking.

We would be okay.

CHAPTER TWENTY-NINE
End of Discussion

Trav's healing took a big leap when we returned from our road trip. An American Boychoir School alumnus sent me an angry letter extolling the Boychoir's virtues, advising me to stop dwelling in the past, and suggesting I spend energy trying to "help build up" the school. However uncommon this letter was in comparison to those from the hundreds of others who have reached out to me in gratitude and solidarity, I have received hate mail like this in the past.

The tone was angry, and the words familiar.

Again, this alumnus did not doubt Trav's experience, but rather, imagined it to be less significant than his own.

But this particular letter prompted a shift in our approach, and instead of me sending my own polite, stock reply, Trav asked to respond.

This ownership marked a turning point, like that moment in Panama City Beach when it was Trav booking the hotel room and asserting his particular needs. Or when he expressed such anger—a man's reaction—that a film would glorify the boy choir experience. When he asked me to review his letter, I felt relief and pride.

There, written in his own words, was a directive that would mark our place in the larger conversation about the effects of childhood sexual abuse. Because I was no longer speaking for Trav, my crippling sense of responsibility began to ease. Reading his draft made me feel not like a parent but like a true partner.

Trav maintains that he is no writer, but his words required no editing, and I think they might be the most powerful sequence in this book.

> *I am glad that you and your friends were not molested and raped while at the American Boychoir School. Some of my friends and I were.*
>
> *Both things are true.*
>
> *I am not a writer, but my wife is, so I asked her to write our story.*
>
> *For decades, the American Boychoir School has prioritized protecting itself as an institution over caring for survivors of abuse perpetrated within that institution.*
>
> *I appreciate that this might make someone currently connected to the school uncomfortable.*
>
> *I do not care.*
>
> *If you or anyone else in your community want to say that my experiences, and the experiences of many others, are less important than your own, then say it to me, not my wife.*

"Say it to me, not my wife."

Trav's voice made our path as a team clear. By owning the narrative, he demonstrates a strength that was once beyond imaginable. No longer a little boy existing in a twisted world of sexual deviance where survival tactics included hiding in the woods or a hallway cabinet, he now accepts the role of a man prepared to speak his truth.

"Just say what happened," our lawyer advised, and that is my advice to any person in this situation. What happened, for us, is that the environment of sexual abuse Trav endured nearly destroyed our marriage. It pushed Trav to the edge of suicide and me to the edge of sanity, and introduced us to mental health diagnoses and treatments I never knew existed. Even today, Trav's experience at the American Boychoir School affects and complicates nearly every decision we make as a couple.

Also true: My husband's dry wit makes me laugh hard. Trav's eyes, the color of Maine's Casco Bay in October, soften when he leans in to listen to me. His strong arms are home, and no man gives a warmer or more welcoming hug.

If a panic attack renders me unable to breathe, Trav is the person I reach for. When he welcomes hardest-case, broken, stray animals into our home—a three-legged dog injured by the force of a speeding car or a scrap of bloated, wormy kitten found near a garbage dumpster—I know these creatures will soon feel safe, loved, and confident, and with Trav's care and commitment, they will heal.

"I can't change what happened to me, Shonna," Trav said when we decided, together, at Maine's Miss Portland Diner to write this book. The server refilled our coffee cups, ran down the list of available pies, and then left while we took a moment to decide. We had just left the lawyer's office, and the Parnassus Books tote bag beside me on the blue upholstered bench seat was stuffed full of American Boychoir School documentation. The enormity of the book-writing task loomed heavy.

"If the only way past it is through it, then let's face it head-on," Trav said, resolute. "Maybe it will do some good."

Pipe & Drape

"**D**o you ever worry about the groupies?"

This, next to "Does he sing to you every day?" is probably the most common question for a musician's wife, and I fielded it from the merchandise table at an Opry-style live revue.

Back on the road for the first time since the epic Americana road trip, we traveled a few hours to the 500-seat venue, and I poked behind the pipe and drape during the sound check, took quick snapshots of the band as they warmed up, and sat with Trav at the plastic table while he charted his songs and the audience began to line up at the door. Two coolers of bottled water and soda cans lined the wall near a large box of potato chips and coffee in plastic urns. Somebody prepared soup and chili, too. The audiovisual guys were rigging up the lights, taping down cords, and testing the sound.

As the crowd found their seats, I spread a cloth to set up the merchandise table while Trav changed into stage wear.

The fan who asked about groupies meant no harm, and I have learned to deflect in a charming, flirtatious manner.

"Oh, I've got plenty of tits and ass," I said with a wink. "I'll start to worry if women show up with cupcakes or offering to do his tax returns."

The fan laughed.

I arranged Trav's table with publicity photos and a rack of *Roadhouse Gospel Hour*, the album born from our winter weeks on the road trip. A collection of Americana standards plus a few healing songs he wrote himself, the project is his proudest recording effort. He booked studio time almost immediately upon our return, and the album contains just his voice accompanied by his dad's Gibson J45.

"Emphasis on the roadhouse," Trav says when fans ask if it is a gospel collection.

"For sinners who sleep late on Sundays," I elaborate. "A forty-five-minute space to set your troubles down."

And to heal, I think, because when Trav walks onstage in his colorful embroidered Western shirt, adjusts his custom leather guitar strap, and strums that first chord on an instrument infused with family history and love—or when his deep, rich voice projects those carefully curated tracks from a purchased recording, particularly his arrangement of the traditional "God's Gonna Cut You Down" popularized by dozens of artists from Odetta to Johnny Cash—I hope listeners believe his lyrics.

I hope listeners applaud or repeat every song on the album, but during this song in particular, when Trav's voice—deep and resonant—sings "What's done in the dark will be brought to the light," I hope listeners, particularly those listeners who suffer with the pervasive effects of childhood sexual abuse, believe those words.

I know I do.

ACKNOWLEDGMENTS

___

I would like to thank the following individuals and organizations, without whom this book would still be an idea too loaded, too frightening, and too overwhelming to contemplate. Trav and I have no idea how we managed to get such good, good people in our orbit, but we are extraordinarily lucky.

First, to Tim and Dorene. Their loving response to Trav's disclosure was an enormous gift. Our entire family, too, both immediate and extended—especially Mom, Dad, Jeff, Ann, Krissy, Douglas, Betsy, Dan, and our nieces and nephews. The Humphrey and Ellis cousins have also been fierce and loyal advocates.

Our community of "we" is broad and includes, in no particular order: Jon and Tara Bossie, Elisabeth Wilkins and Joe Lombardo, Anne Mommsen, Cathy Kidman and Ramona Morrissette, Brooke Williams and Chris Burke, Erin Irish, Todd and Beth Wagstaff, Beth Ahlgren and Matt Bohn, Ruth and Mark Smith, Jessica and Brendan

Gilpatrick, Robert Vilas, Sara Litwiller, Marsea Spiegel, Tom Ambrose, Per Hanson, Will Jones, Ralph Sordyl, Bret Boydston, Terri and Tyler Patterson, and Carson Lynch. My longtime reader friends, too: Ruthie, Laurie, Amy, Jamie, Heather, Agustina, Michelle, Ryl, Kim, and Maya.

The Gorham Grind and the Big Island lava flow hale, where I sketched out the concept, played a large role in this book's construction. Thomas College, especially the Advancement team, afforded me the space and encouragement to proceed while also earning a salary. Chris Anderson and Steve LePore reached out to us on behalf of MaleSurvivor.org and 1in6.org, respectively, and the lady from Courthouse Dogs likely has no idea that her note to us prompted one of the most pivotal moments in Trav's healing. These are good, good people.

To Lawrence Lessig, whom I have never met in person, for having the courage and tenacity to model that the negative American Boychoir School experience need not define a man. To Chris Dinan and Brenda Buchanan for their wise counsel. To the *Atlantic* editor who bought my first essay and to the Salon editor who bought and sharpened my second one. To my agent, Stephany Evans, for helping find this book a home, and to Nancy Schenck and Valerie Killeen at Central Recovery Press for shaping this material into book form.

Finally, and most importantly, to the victims of childhood sexual abuse and their families: Please know that you are loved. You are loved, you matter, and you are so much more than this terrible thing that happened. Please have the courage to steer that van off the highway. Places like Nashville's Loveless Café make some fine biscuits, and it would be a shame for you to miss them.

RESURCES

The following are reprinted with permission from 1in6 and Male Survivor. Although different in scope and mission, both are organizations that help men who have experienced sex abuse. Both can be instrumental agents in healing. More information and resources are available at www.1in6.org and www.malesurvivor.org.

The One in Six Statistic

Yes, it is hard to believe. There's strong scientific evidence.

Researchers have found that one in six men have experienced abusive sexual experiences before age eighteen. And this is probably a low estimate, since it doesn't include noncontact experiences, which can also have lasting negative effects.

If you've had such an experience, or think you might have, you are not alone.

If you wonder whether such an experience may be connected to some difficulties or challenges in your life now, you are not alone.

Whoever you are, maybe you're thinking something like "One in six! Come on, how can that be?" or even "That can't be true!" Again, if so, you're not alone. Those are common responses to this statistic, which many people find hard to believe—including men who've had such experiences themselves.

This information is about saying, briefly, "Yes, it is hard to believe," and "There's strong scientific evidence."

Please note:

- Researchers use "sexual abuse" to describe experiences in which children are subjected to *unwanted sexual contact involving force, threats, or a large age difference* between the child and the other person (which involves a big power differential and exploitation). See former advisory board member Dr. Jim Hopper's "Sexual Abuse of Males" for a detailed discussion of definitions and research methods, including how some result in lower estimates than one in six (e.g., large national surveys using telephone interviews with few questions).

- Having such an experience does not mean a boy will definitely suffer significant long-term negative consequences. That depends on several factors, including how many times it happened, how long it went on, who else was involved, whether the boy told anyone and, if so, the response he received.

What the Research Tells Us

- A 2005 study conducted by the US Centers for Disease Control and Prevention, on San Diego Kaiser Permanente HMO members, reported that 16 percent of males were sexually abused by the age of eighteen.

- A 2003 national study of US adults reported that 14.2 percent of men were sexually abused before the age of eighteen.

- A 1998 study reviewing research on male childhood sexual abuse concluded that the problems are "common, under-reported, under-recognized, and under-treated."

- A 1996 study of male university students in the Boston area reported that 18 percent of men were sexually abused before the age of sixteen.

- A 1990 national study of US adults reported that 16 percent of men were sexually abused before the age of eighteen.

Why These Statistics Are Probably Underestimates

- Males who have such experiences are less likely to disclose them than are females.

- Only 16 percent of men with documented histories of sexual abuse (by social service agencies, which means it was very serious) considered themselves to have been sexually abused, compared to 64 percent of women with documented histories in the same study.

Men who've had such experiences are at much greater risk than those who haven't for serious mental health problems, including:

- Symptoms of post-traumatic stress disorder and depression.

- Alcoholism and drug abuse.
- Suicidal thoughts and suicide attempts.
- Problems in intimate relationships.
- Underachievement at school and at work.

Think about it, and about educating others.

In summary, the one in six statistic is supported by solid scientific research, including a study conducted by the US Centers for Disease Control and Prevention, and is likely an underestimate of the actual prevalence. Furthermore, this widespread problem contributes to mental health and personal and work difficulties of many men.

Yet few people are aware there are just as many men who experienced sexual abuse as children as there are who develop prostate cancer, the most common cancer and second leading cause of death among men. And few know that the nineteen million men with histories of childhood sexual abuse are *more than four times* the number with heart disease, the leading cause of death among men.

MALE SEXUAL VICTIMIZATION MYTHS & FACTS

Myth №1: Boys and men can't be victims.

This myth, instilled through masculine gender socialization and sometimes referred to as the "macho image," declares that males, even young boys, are not supposed to be victims or even vulnerable. We learn very early that males should be able to protect themselves.

In truth, boys are children—weaker and more vulnerable than their perpetrators—who cannot really fight back. Why? The perpetrator has greater size, strength, and knowledge. This power is exercised from a position of authority, using resources such as money or other bribes, or outright threats—whatever advantage can be taken to use a child for sexual purposes.

Myth №2: Most sexual abuse of boys is perpetrated by homosexual males.

Pedophiles who molest boys are not expressing a homosexual orientation any more than pedophiles who molest girls are practicing heterosexual behaviors. While many child molesters have gender and/ or age preferences, of those who seek out boys, the vast majority are not homosexual. They are pedophiles.

Myth №3: If a boy experiences sexual arousal or orgasm from abuse, this means he was a willing participant or enjoyed it.

In reality, males can respond physically to stimulation (get an erection) even in traumatic or painful sexual situations. Therapists who work with sexual offenders know that one way a perpetrator can maintain secrecy is to label the child's sexual response as an indication of his willingness to participate. "You liked it, you wanted it," they'll say.

Many survivors feel guilt and shame because they experienced physical arousal while being abused. Physical (and visual or auditory) stimulation is likely to happen in a sexual situation. It does not mean the child wanted the experience or understood what it meant at the time.

Myth №4: Boys are less traumatized by the abuse experience than girls.

While some studies have found males to be less negatively affected, more studies show that long-term effects are quite damaging for either sex. Males may be more damaged by society's refusal or reluctance to accept their victimization, and by their resultant belief that they must "tough it out" in silence.

Myth №5: Boys abused by males are or will become homosexual.

While there are different theories about how the sexual orientation develops, experts in the human sexuality field do not believe that premature sexual experiences play a significant role in late adolescent or adult sexual orientation. It is unlikely that someone can make another person a homosexual or heterosexual. Sexual orientation is a complex issue and there is no single answer or theory that explains why someone identifies himself as homosexual, heterosexual, or bisexual.

Whether perpetrated by older males or females, boys' or girls' premature sexual experiences are damaging in many ways, including confusion about one's sexual identity and orientation.

Many boys who have been abused by males erroneously believe that something about them sexually attracts males, and that this may mean they are homosexual or effeminate. Again, not true. Pedophiles who are attracted to boys will admit that the lack of body hair and adult sexual features turn them on. The pedophile's inability to develop and maintain a healthy adult sexual relationship is the problem, not the physical features of a sexually immature boy.

Myth №6: The "Vampire Syndrome," that is, boys who are sexually abused, like the victims of Count Dracula, go on to "bite" or sexually abuse others.

This myth is especially dangerous because it can create a terrible stigma for the child that he is destined to become an offender. Boys might be treated as potential perpetrators rather than victims who need help. While it is true that most perpetrators have histories of sexual abuse, it is *not* true that most victims go on to become perpetrators.

Research by Jane Gilgun, Judith Becker, and John Hunter found a primary difference between perpetrators who were sexually abused and sexually abused males who never perpetrated: Non-perpetrators told about the abuse, and were believed and supported by significant people in their lives. Again, the majority of victims do not go on to become adolescent or adult perpetrators; and those who do perpetrate in adolescence usually don't perpetrate as adults if they get help when they are young.

Myth №7: If the perpetrator is female, the boy or adolescent should consider himself fortunate to have been initiated into heterosexual activity.

In reality, premature or coerced sex, whether by a mother, aunt, older sister, babysitter, or other female in a position of power over a boy, causes confusion at best, and rage, depression, or other problems in more negative circumstances. To be used as a sexual object by a more powerful person, male or female, is always abusive and often damaging.

Believing these myths is dangerous and damaging.

- So long as people believe these myths, and larger society teaches them to children from their earliest years, sexually abused males will be unlikely to get the recognition and help they need.
- So long as people believe these myths, sexually abused males will be more likely to join the minority of survivors who perpetuate this suffering by abusing others.
- So long as boys or men who have been sexually abused believe these myths, they will feel ashamed and angry.
- And so long as sexually abused males believe these myths, they reinforce the power of another devastating myth that all abused children struggle with: that it was their fault. It is never the fault of the child in a sexual situation, though perpetrators can be quite

skilled at getting their victims to believe these myths and take on responsibility that is always and only their own.

———

For any male who has been sexually abused, becoming free of these myths is an essential part of the recovery process.

Also Available from Central Recovery Press

BEHAVIORAL HEALTH

Self-Acceptance: The Key to Recovery from Mental Illness
Victor Ashear, PhD with Vanessa Hastings | $24.95 US
ISBN: 978-1-937612-91-7 | E-book: 978-1-937612-92-4

Engage the Group, Engage the Brain:
100 Experiential Activities for Addiction Treatment
Kay Colbert, LCSW and Roxanna Erickson-Klein, PhD, LPC | $26.95 US
ISBN: 978-1-937612-89-4 | E-book: 978-1-937612-90-0

Irrelationship: How We Use Dysfunctional Relationships to Hide from Intimacy
Mark Borg, Jr., PhD; Grant Brenner, MD; Daniel Berry, RN, MHA
$16.95 US | ISBN: 978-1-942094-00-5 | E-book: 978-1-942094-01-2

All Bets Are Off: Losers, Liars, and Recovery from Gambling Addiction
Arnie and Sheila Wexler with Steve Jacobson | $16.95 US
ISBN: 978-1-937612-75-7 | E-book: 978-1-937612-76-4

Wisdom from the Couch: Knowing and Growing Yourself from the Inside Out
Jennifer L. Kunst, PhD | $16.95 US | ISBN: 978-1-937612-61-0
E-book: 978-1-937612-62-7

Hard to Love: Understanding and Overcoming
Male Borderline Personality Disorder
Joseph Nowinski, PhD | $15.95 US | ISBN: 978-1-937612-57-3
E-book: 978-1-937612-58-0

Many Faces, One Voice: Secrets from The Anonymous People
Bud Mikhitarian | $17.95 US | ISBN: 978-1-937612-93-1 | E-book: 978-1-937612-94-8

A Man's Way through Relationships: Learning to Love and Be Loved
Dan Griffin, MA | $15.95 US | ISBN: 978-1-937612-66-5 | E-book: 978-1-937612-67-2

Disentangle: When You've Lost Your Self in Someone Else
Nancy L. Johnston, MS, LPC, LSATP | $15.95 US
ISBN: 978-1-936290-03-1 | E-book: 978-1-936290-49-9

Game Plan: A Man's Guide to Achieving Emotional Fitness
Alan P Lyme, LCSW; David J Powell, PhD; Stephen R Andrew, LCSW | $15.95 US
ISBN: 978-1-936290-96-3 | E-book: 978-1-937612-04-7

The Light Side of the Moon: Reclaiming Your Lost Potential
Ditta M Oliker, PhD | $16.95 US | ISBN: 978-1-936290-95-6 | E-book: 978-1-937612-03-0

INSPIRATIONAL

The Wisdom of a Meaningful Life: The Essence of Mindfulness
John Bruna | $15.95 US | ISBN: 978-1-942094-18-0 | E-book: 978-1-942094-19-7

I Don't Know What to Believe: Making Spiritual Peace with Your Religion
Rabbi Ben Kamin | $16.95 US | ISBN: 978-1-942094-04-3 | E-book: 978-1-942094-05-0

The Truth Begins with You: Reflections to Heal Your Spirit
Claudia Black, PhD | $17.95 US | ISBN: 978-1-936290-61-1 | E-book: 978-1-936290-78-9

CAREGIVING
The Family Caregiver's Manual:
A Practical Planning Guide to Managing the Care of Your Loved One
David Levy, JD, Gerontologist | $24.95 US | ISBN: 978-1-942094-12-8
E-book: 978-1-942094-13-5

Love in the Land of Dementia: Finding Hope in the Caregiver's Journey
Deborah Shouse | $15.95 US | ISBN: 978-1-937612-49-8 | E-book: 978-1-937612-50-4

Dancing in the Dark: How to Take Care of Yourself
When Someone You Love Is Depressed
Bernadette Stankard and Amy Viets | $15.95 US | ISBN: 978-1-936290-70-3
E-book: 978-1-936290-83-3

MEMOIRS
Never Leave Your Dead: A True Story of War Trauma, Murder, and Madness
Diane Cameron | $15.95 US | ISBN: 978-1-942094-16-6 | E-book: 978-1-942094-17-3

The Jaguar Man: A Memoir
Lara Naughton | $15.95 US | ISBN: 978-1-942094-20-3 | E-book: 978-1-942094-21-0

Bottled: A Mom's Guide to Early Recovery
Dana Bowman | $16.95 US | ISBN: 978-1-937612-97-9 | E-book: 978-1-937612-98-6

Body Punishment: OCD, Addiction, and Finding the Courage to Heal
Maggie Lamond Simone | $15.95 US | ISBN: 978-1-937612-81-8
E-book: 978-1-937612-82-5

Weightless: My Life as a Fat Man and How I Escaped
Gregg McBride | $17.95 US | ISBN: 978-1-937612-69-6 | E-book: 978-1-937612-70-2

Acrobaddict
Joe Putignano | $17.95 US | ISBN: 978-1-937612-51-1 | E-book: 978-1-937612-52-8

Rage: The Legend of "Baseball Bill" Denehy
Bill Denehy with Peter Golenbock | $16.95 US | ISBN: 978-1-937612-55-9
E-book: 978-1-937612-56-6

From Harvard to Hell . . . and Back:
A Doctor's Journey through Addiction to Recovery
Sylvester "Skip" Sviokla III, MD with Kerry Zukus | $16.95 US
ISBN: 978-937612-29-0 | E-book: 978-1-937612-30-6

Dark Wine Waters: My Husband of a Thousand Joys and Sorrows
Fran Simone, PhD | $15.95 US | ISBN: 978-1-937612-64-1 | E-book: 978-1-937612-65-8

Finding a Purpose in the Pain: A Doctor's Approach to Addiction Recovery and Healing
James L Finley, Jr., MD | $15.95 US | ISBN: 978-1-936290-71-0
E-book: 978-1-936290-84-0

The Mindful Addict: A Memoir of the Awakening of a Spirit
Tom Catton | $18.95 US | ISBN: 978-0-9818482-7-3 | E-book: 978-1-936290-44-4

Some Assembly Required: A Balanced Approach to Recovery
from Addiction and Chronic Pain
Dan Mager, MSW | $16.95 US | ISBN: 978-1-937612-25-2 | E-book: 978-1-937612-26-9

RELATIONSHIPS AND RECOVERY
Making Peace with Your Plate: Eating Disorder Recovery
Robyn Cruze and Espra Andrus, LCSW | $16.95 US | ISBN: 978-1-937612-45-0
E-book: 978-1-937612-46-7

Loving Our Addicted Daughters Back to Life: A Guidebook for Parents
Linda Dahl | $16.95 US | ISBN: 978-1-937612-85-6 | E-book: 978-1-937612-86-3

The Joey Song: A Mother's Story of Her Son's Addiction
Sandra Swenson | $15.95 US | ISBN: 978-1-937612-71-9 | E-book: 978-1-937612-72-6

Out of the Woods: A Woman's Guide to Long-Term Recovery
Diane Cameron | $15.95 US | ISBN: 978-1-937612-47-4 | E-book: 978-1-937612-48-1

May I Sit with You: A Simple Approach to Meditation
Tom Catton | $15.95 US | ISBN: 978-1-937612-83-2 | E-book: 978-1-937612-84-9

REFERENCE
Behavioral Addiction: Screening, Assessment, and Treatment
An-Pyng Sun, PhD; Larry Ashley, EdS; Lesley Dickson, MD | $18.95 US
ISBN: 978-1-936290-97-0 | E-book: 978-1-937612-05-4

When the Servant Becomes the Master: A Comprehensive Addiction Guide for
Those Who Suffer from the Disease, the Loved Ones Affected by It,
and the Professionals Who Assist Them
Jason Z W Powers, MD | $18.95 US | ISBN: 978-1-936290-73-4
E-book: 978-1-936290-86-4